A PROJECT BY
CITY OF COMMERCE PUBLIC LIBRARY

COMMERCE NOW

ONE CITY, MANY STORIES

Commerce Now
© 2026
ISBN: 978-1-966337-30-0

First Edition, 2026

Printed in the United States of America

Cover Design by: Josué Martínez
Layout Design by: Erica Castro

This book is dedicated to all the people, past and present, who have made this city a place we can all call home.

Table of Contents

Mayor Kevin Lainez
(2026)

In the summer of 2012, my lovely wife Elisa had just given birth to our oldest son, Roman, and we were searching for a place where our growing family could plant its roots. We wanted a community that was central, safe, and built on strong family values. When we came across Commerce, our search immediately came to an end. We were absolutely enamored with the parks, libraries, youth programs, community events, and most importantly, the people. Coming from a larger city like Los Angeles, while all of these things are present, what is often missing is the sense of connection. Commerce is a truly tight-knit community.

Another son (Milo) and a dog (Espooky) later, I can honestly say that moving here was one of the best decisions I've ever made. Our sons are both active in the parks programs, our amazing City employees continue to collaborate to create community events and excursions that allow our family to build lifelong memories, and our neighbors are friendly, supportive, and considerate. Oh, and did I mention Camp Commerce??? I'm proud to have joined the club who are proud to call the City of Commerce home.

As you read through Commerce Now, you'll come to many realizations, but there are two truths that stand out:

1) The City of Commerce is a great City.
2) Its greatness is only possible because of the people that inhabit it.

This collection of interviews is a celebration of those very people - the neighbors, families, employees, and leaders whose stories reflect the heart of our community. I hope their voices remind you, as they remind me every day, why Commerce is such a special place to be.

— Mayor Kevin Lainez, 2026

Mayor Ivan Altamirano
(2025)

As I look around our city today, I am filled with pride for what Commerce has become a place where creativity, culture, and community are coming together like never before. Our residents are embracing a new chapter through the Arts District, where murals are transforming blank walls into vibrant stories. Each brushstroke tells a piece of our journey, our history, our dreams, and our unity. These works of art are more than decoration; they're the new foundation of who we are and who we're becoming. Commerce is evolving into a city where art inspires connection, where color meets purpose, and where our shared vision for the future continues to rise with every wall we paint.

— Mayor Ivan Altamirano, 2025

Introduction

Those of us fortunate enough to work at the library, sometimes hear "origin" stories of the City of Commerce. The area had previously been considered part of unincorporated Los Angeles County. Residents, however, were dissatisfied with the services they had been receiving from the county and even more upset to learn about impending cuts to library services. In response, residents boldly joined forces to put their future in their own hands. The City of Commerce was born (incorporated) on January 28, 1960.

The events are chronicled in two books: *City of Commerce: An Enterprising Heritage* and *Commerce Then: From an Oral History of the Lives of Eight Residents of Commerce, California.* It's been 35 years since these books were published, so it seemed like a good time to see what our residents have been up to. So, residents were invited to share their stories, either in writing, or via interviews. What follows is a selection of entries from residents of all ages.

In putting this anthology together, we did our best to respect our authors' words. Sometimes, though, for the sake of clarity or narrative flow, we may have made minor edits. The Library is extremely grateful to those of you who shared your stories and for those of you taking the time to read them. The stories of our residents, employees, and businesses form the story of our city.

Happy Reading!

--The Commerce Now Team

The Heart of the City
El corazón de la ciudad

Raúl Elenes

Don Raúl: The Heart of the City

Raúl Elenes has lived in Commerce for forty-five years, yet his story stretches far beyond the city's borders, carrying the rhythm of history, resilience, and a life devoted to service. To meet him is to meet a man whose presence seems to fill the streets with memory, laughter, and a quiet authority born from decades of dedication.

When Raúl first arrived in Commerce, the city was a different place. Streets that now brim with safety and light were once shadowed by fear. "The cholos from Bell Gardens would gather here," he recalls, voice steady but eyes flickering with memory. "They had gatherings in the streets, drugs… you couldn't even drive at night."

But Raúl was not one to cower. He joined the Neighborhood Watch, reporting incidents, walking the streets, and slowly reshaping the neighborhood with nothing but persistence and courage. "They realized I wasn't afraid anymore," he says. One evening, a tense standoff ended with local police enforcing order, and Raúl remembers a veteran named Salvador, perched on a low wall, witnessing the city's transformation unfold.

Raúl's life in Commerce began with a simple, profoundly human desire: to give his wife a place to plant her garden. Moving from an apartment surrounded by concrete in Maywood, they found a yard in Commerce wide enough for her passion. That garden became the first root of Raúl's deeper connection to the city—a connection that would grow into decades of civic engagement.

He became a fixture in local government, volunteering for city council campaigns, serving over twenty years as a commissioner for seniors, and taking part in traffic commissions to prevent accidents in his neighborhood. "We worked with Bell Gardens to put in a left turn lane. No more accidents since then," he says matter-of-factly, as if decades of service could be summed up in a single traffic signal.

Yet, his contributions extended far beyond regulations and committees. Raúl has spent more than thirty years distributing food to seniors, organizing events, arranging transportation, and lifting the spirits of those around him. "I feel good serving the people and the city," he says. For him, volunteering is not a duty—it is a way of life, a therapy, a means of keeping body and mind active.

Through all this, Raúl has witnessed the transformation of Commerce. The city has grown, built new parks, added bus shelters, and developed thriving commercial centers. "The Citadel changed everything," he says, eyes sparkling. "It brought people together from all over, friends, families. Commerce became bigger, safer, more welcoming."

At home, Raúl's legacy is equally rich. He lived fifty-five years with his beloved wife, raising two sons and two daughters. Today, he has seven grandchildren and a host of great-grandchildren, each carrying a piece of his values forward. Even at ninety-eight, he remains vibrant, attending dances, organizing trips, and encouraging others to stay active. "The secret," he says, "is to never sit down and do nothing. Keep active, keep helping, and life will carry you forward."

For Don Raúl, the measure of a life well-lived is service. "I like to serve people and the city," he says simply. His legacy is not in monuments or accolades, though he has many trophies to show for his decades of volunteerism. His true legacy is in the streets he helped clean, the lives he touched, and the city he helped transform. Commerce, he believes, is not just a place to live—it is a community to nurture, a story to be shared, and a gift to be passed to future generations.

In a city that has changed so much over the years, Don Raúl remains a constant: a living testament to dedication, kindness, and the quiet power of one person to shape the world around them.

Don Raúl: El corazón de la ciudad

Raúl Elenes ha vivido en Commerce durante cuarenta y cinco años, pero su historia se extiende mucho más allá de los límites de la ciudad, llevando consigo el ritmo de la historia, la resiliencia y una vida dedicada al servicio. Conocerlo es encontrarse con un hombre cuya presencia parece llenar las calles de memoria, risas y una autoridad serena nacida de décadas de entrega.

Cuando Raúl llegó por primera vez a Commerce, la ciudad era muy distinta. Calles que hoy están llenas de luz y seguridad antes estaban marcadas por el miedo. "Los cholos de Bell Gardens se juntaban aquí", recuerda, con la voz firme y los ojos encendidos por la memoria. "Había celebraciones en media calle, drogas... ni siquiera se podía manejar de noche".

Pero Raúl no era de los que se escondían. Se unió al Comité de Seguridad Vecinal, comenzó a reportar incidentes, a recorrer las calles y, poco a poco, a transformar el vecindario con nada más que constancia y valentía. "Se dieron cuenta de que ya no tenía miedo", dice. Una noche, un enfrentamiento tenso terminó cuando la policía local impuso el orden, y Raúl recuerda a un veterano llamado Salvador, sentado sobre una bardita baja, presenciando cómo la ciudad empezaba a cambiar.

La vida de Raúl en Commerce comenzó con un deseo sencillo y profundamente humano: darle a su esposa un lugar donde pudiera plantar su jardín. Después de vivir en un departamento rodeado de cemento en Maywood, encontraron en Commerce un patio lo suficientemente grande para su pasión. Ese jardín se convirtió en la primera raíz de la profunda conexión de Raúl con la ciudad, una conexión que crecería hasta convertirse en décadas de participación cívica.

Se volvió una figura constante en el gobierno local, apoyando campañas del concejo municipal, sirviendo por más de veinte años como comisionado de adultos mayores y participando en comisiones de tráfico para prevenir accidentes en su vecindario. "Trabajamos con Bell Gardens para poner un carril de vuelta a la izquierda. Desde entonces ya no ha habido accidentes", dice con sencillez, como si décadas de servicio pudieran resumirse en una sola señal de tránsito.

Sin embargo, sus aportaciones fueron mucho más allá de reglamentos y comités. Raúl ha pasado más de treinta años ayudando en la distribución de alimentos para los adultos mayores, organizando eventos, coordinando transportación y levantando el ánimo de quienes lo rodean. "Me siento bien sirviendo a la gente y a la ciudad", dice. Para él, el voluntariado no es una obligación: es una forma de vida, una terapia, una manera de mantener el cuerpo y la mente activos.

A lo largo de los años, Raúl ha sido testigo de la transformación de Commerce. La ciudad creció, construyó nuevos parques, agregó paradas de autobús y desarrolló centros comerciales prósperos. "El Citadel lo cambió todo", dice con los ojos brillantes. "Trajo gente de todas partes, amigos, familias. Commerce se hizo más grande, más segura, más acogedora".

En casa, el legado de Raúl es igual de profundo. Vivió cincuenta y cinco años con su amada esposa, con quien formó una familia de dos hijos y dos hijas. Hoy tiene siete nietos y numerosos bisnietos, cada uno llevando consigo un pedacito de sus valores. Incluso a los noventa y ocho años, sigue lleno de vida: asiste a bailes, organiza paseos y anima a otros a mantenerse activos. "El secreto —dice— es nunca sentarse a no hacer nada. Hay que seguir activos, seguir ayudando, y la vida sola te va llevando".

Para Don Raúl, la medida de una vida bien vivida es el servicio. "Me gusta servir a la gente y a la ciudad", dice con sencillez. Su legado no está en monumentos ni reconocimientos, aunque tiene muchos trofeos que recuerdan sus décadas de voluntariado. Su verdadero legado está en las calles que a ayudadó a limpiar, en las vidas que a tocado y en la ciudad que a ayudadó a transformar. Commerce, cree él, no es solo un lugar para vivir: es una comunidad que se debe cuidar, una historia que se debe compartir y un regalo que se pasa a las futuras generaciones.

En una ciudad que ha cambiado tanto con los años, Don Raúl permanece constante: es un testimonio vivo de la dedicación, la bondad y el poder silencioso de una sola persona que transforma el mundo que lo rodea.

A Life in Commerce: The Story of Jesús "Jesse" Quintero

Jesús Quintero

A Life in Commerce: The Story of Jesús "Jesse" Quintero

Jesús Quintero has spent nearly his entire life in the heart of the City of Commerce. To those who have walked through the doors of the Commerce Public Library, he is more than just the friendly face behind the front desk—he is part of the city's living memory. His story intertwines the history of a community with the quiet dedication of a man who has spent decades helping others learn, connect, and belong.

"I was four years old when my family moved from City Terrace to Commerce in 1964," Jesse recalls. "My dad had just bought our first house—a four-bedroom place big enough for all ten of us kids." Commerce was still a young city then, having incorporated only four years earlier, the same year Jesse was born. "I guess you could say we grew up together," he smiles. He remembers his earliest days clearly: "I started preschool at Ford Boulevard Elementary. My sister would walk me to school, drop me off, and go home. One day, by the time she got back home, I was already there. I'd walked myself home." It's a story that captures the spirit of the time—when neighborhoods were safe, kids roamed freely, and everyone knew each other. "We didn't have many cars, but we had a lot of heart," Jesse says.

As a child, Jesse quickly found joy and belonging in the city's parks. "When I was six, I played baseball at Bristow Park. I was one of the smallest kids on the team, but that year I won the trophy for Best Sportsmanship." He still remembers being honored at a Commerce City Council meeting in 1966, his photo appearing in the *Commerce Tribune*. "That was huge for me," he says. "It made me feel seen." For Jesse, that sense of recognition—being valued by his community—became something he carried throughout his life.

Jesse's lifelong connection to libraries began when illness kept him home from school. "I had the chickenpox and measles at the same time. I couldn't go to class, so I spent my days at the small trailer library at Northwest Park, which is now Bristow Park. I was six years old, surrounded by books—and I fell in love." Years later, that love became his life's work. "I've worked in libraries all my life—city libraries, county libraries. Even when I was working full-time at the Los Angeles Department of Water and Power, I missed it." When his sister Laura told him the Commerce Library was hiring, he jumped at the chance. "I thought, why not? I can work part-time and get back to what I love." He started as a Library Page and was soon promoted to Library Assistant. "I've been here almost thirty years now, everyone in Commerce knows me. It's like family," he says proudly.

Before returning to his hometown roots, Jesse served three years in the U.S. Army. "I joined when I turned twenty," he explains. "That experience taught me discipline and pride in service—values that carried into everything I did afterward." After his military service, Jesse worked for the Los Angeles Department of Water and Power for thirty-one years, retiring nearly a decade ago. But even while managing a full-time career, he never stopped working part-time for Commerce. "Eighteen years of double duty," he laughs. "That's how much I love this city."

Over six decades, Jesse has seen Commerce change and grow. "Back in the '60s, the city was very neighborhood-oriented," he says. "You had Bristow, Rosewood, Quigley (now Veterans), and Bandini—each had its own identity. Over time, though, we've become more connected. The free buses helped with that. The parks, the libraries—they brought people together." He still re-members the early days of the city's Halloween parades. "In 1967 or '68, I dressed up as Robin Hood—green leotards and all," he laughs. "I won a Batman board game that year and was presented my prize at City Hall." Sports, community events, and a strong civic pride were—and still are—part of the city's DNA. "Commerce recognizes people," Jesse says. "They make you feel like you matter."

Speaking with deep affection, Jesse describes the place that shaped him: "Commerce has always been the model city. It was built to be an example—a place where people could live, work, and raise families without losing that small-town heart." He's quick to mention the city's most famous perks. "Our buses are still free. People from other cities can't believe it," he laughs. "They come to our library, and they say, 'You guys have such nice services.' And I tell them, that's Commerce. We do it right."

For Jesse, being part of Commerce means giving back. "Since childhood, this city gave me so much—a safe place to grow up, teachers and coaches who cared, and a community that looked out for one another. Working at the library is my way of returning that kindness." Helping others, he believes, is at the heart of what makes Commerce special. "It's so fulfilling to make a difference in someone's life, even in small ways. That's what I love most."

Reflecting on decades gone by, Jesse's message to future generations is simple but powerful: "Keep giving back. Things change—buildings, roads, even technology—but kindness and community should never fade. Help people. That's what keeps a city alive." He smiles when asked if he ever plans to leave Commerce. "No," he says without hesitation. "This has always been home. I might take the occasional trip to Vegas, but I'll always come back here."

Because for Jesús Quintero, the City of Commerce isn't just where he lives—it is who he is.

Signs and Castles

Gloria Nezahualcóyotl

Signs and Castles

The one thing I remember from my first bus ride from Tijuana to Los Angeles was the City of Commerce baseball stadium scoreboard. That might seem odd to you, but it was just like the one in Angel Flores Stadium in Culiacán. It reminded me of home, while welcoming me to this new place. I was making a mental note to share this with my family, when the Citadel building suddenly appeared before my eyes. I wondered what mysteries this castle held.

This sign and the castle became my main topics of conversation for some time, with the castle symbolizing an unknown future to be explored. My family lived in the Pico-Union area at the time. It would take two years for us to move closer to Commerce, in the East Los Angeles area. My relatives were referred for work at the Citadel, since it was considered to be a safe place. They stayed there for a while, before moving on to other jobs.

Once we were free to travel between the two countries, I kept my eye on the baseball stadium scoreboard every time we drove by. At the time I was told that the Dodgers practiced there, but I never visited the stadium.

When the City of Commerce purchased then sold the Citadel property, I was happy to hear that the façade was going to be saved. So much history decorated the walls, and there was even more behind them.

Years later, I had the opportunity to move into a home a few yards from the stadium. There I would see high school and neighbor-hood games.

Once the Citadel Outlets opened, I would admire the effort that was made to preserve as much of it as possible.

Today, the scoreboard is gone, the baseball field has been ripped apart, the bleachers are unusable, and the future of the site remains unknown. It makes me sad, angry, and disappointed, all at the same time. But I remain in awe of the Citadel and its thriving businesses.

Where the Doors Are Always Open

Yvonne Sandoval

Where the Doors Are Always Open

On most mornings in the City of Commerce, just before the clock strikes ten, a familiar voice carries through the Senior Center lobby.

"Hey, everybody!"

It is not loud in a disruptive way. It is declarative. A small announcement of presence. A refusal to let a room remain anonymous.

The woman behind that voice is Yvonne Sandoval, and for forty years she has been practicing the simple, radical art of showing up.

Yvonne did not arrive in Commerce with ambition for leadership or recognition. She arrived with her husband, three children, and a decision. "Find us a house," she told a real estate agent. When the right one appeared, she did not hesitate. Yvonne took the keys. They moved in on the day of her youngest daughter's birthday. That same day, they went to a shelter and adopted a dog named Rio. It felt like putting down permanent roots. What she did not yet understand was that Commerce was not merely a place to live. It was a place that invited participation.

The first city flyer she received caught her attention—parks, programs, and teams. Yvonne told her husband, "I'll be right back," and drove to Rosewood Park. Her oldest daughter, then eleven, was doing somersaults in the park, while Yvonne filled out registration forms. A coach glanced at the girl and said, "I need her on my team."

That was how it began.

One practice became two. Volleyball became basketball. Soon there were T-ball games for the younger two children, carpools, tournaments, and All-Star seasons. Yvonne became the kind of mother who could pivot mid-conversation, smile, and say, "Sorry, gotta go," before hurrying to the next field, the next gym, or the next pickup.

Yvonne and her husband learned to divide the city like choreography—he would take one child to practice, she would take another. They met coaches in parking lots, drove to games across Southern California, and built their family calendar around whistles and scoreboards. When her husband passed away in 1998, the rhythm changed. There was grief, and there was work. There were children still growing. She kept moving. The city's programs—its schools, its parks, its traditions—became her support system.

Her roots, however, reached deeper than Commerce. She had grown up in East Los Angeles, shaped by parish life at Our Lady of Guadalupe. Her father was an usher—disciplined, visible, devoted. He helped organize pancake breakfasts to fund the school and stood proudly during the annual procession down Brooklyn Avenue, before it was renamed César Chávez. She remembered waiting as other parishes joined, banners raised, each carrying a different name for the Virgin Mary from across Latin America. Faith, community, identity—they were not abstractions. They were lived in the body. Service, she realizes now, is inherited.

Years later, standing masked among a crowd commemorating the Chicano Moratorium, she felt something awaken again. As a girl, her parents had once allowed her to attend a small protest connected to César Chávez. They had not permitted more, but the memory lingered. When she walked in 2020 among thousands, she understood that participation in civic life does not require a title. It requires presence, which would define her next chapter.

The turning point came, fittingly, at the library. A flyer advertised a mental health event. She attended out of curiosity and left with purpose. For years, her husband's PTSD had been something doctors advised the family not to discuss. "Don't tell anybody," they had said. In the 1980s, there had been no common language for anxiety, no open conversations about trauma. Silence was mistaken for strength. Yvonne decided to break that silence.

She trained as a peer support specialist through Project Return and began facilitating groups—one in person, another online. Through a modest website, she found herself speaking not only to residents of Commerce but to participants in Greece, Portugal, and beyond. Professionals joined, strangers joined, and people looking for what she called "sunlight."

She discovered something else along the way: seniors, too, suffer quietly. The revelation came unexpectedly. One morning, arriving for exercise, she realized the machines had been moved to the aquatics center. With an unexpected hour to spare, she wandered into a Senior Center club meeting. She sat at a table, introduced herself, mentioned the support groups she facilitated, and conversations began.

She would later become secretary of one club and president of another. When she assumed leadership, the treasury stood at zero; previous funds had been donated elsewhere. They organized membership drives, bus trips and sought modest dues. This led to coffee at ten o'clock and three dollar lunches.

"Five generations," she tells them during meetings, looking around at faces in their fifties, sixties, seventies, eighties, even nineties. "We are holding space." She believes in laughter as medicine. She believes in naming grief before it hardens. Yvonne believes that change—retirement, relocation, the death of friends—can disorient even the strongest among them. She listens, teases, and makes sure no one sits too long in silence.

Commerce itself has changed over her forty years. Day camp that was once free now carries a fee. Resident cards come in tiers. Flyers that once arrived rolled and tucked into fences have been replaced by apps and social media. Buses now connect the city to downtown Los Angeles and California State University, Los Angeles, expanding possibilities for students who once relied on their parents' cars. Yet some things remain constant.

Camp Commerce still gathers families in winter snow and summer heat. Children still sprint across park fields. Coaches still call out instructions. The library still opens doors into wider worlds. Yvonne speaks of the city with affection but also with humility. "We must stay humble," she says. "Be part of the solution. Not the problem." Indeed, she resists the idea that residents are spoiled by good services. Instead, she sees responsibility: to participate in decision-making, to attend meetings, and to ensure that programs continue.

She speaks easily with council members and remembers when city leaders traveled to Washington, D.C. in 1965 to secure resources for the community. She understands that what exists today was built deliberately.

When asked how she would like future generations to remember Commerce, she gently rejects the premise. "They won't have to remember," she says. "It will still continue to exist." Existence, for her, is sustained by involvement. By getting up and leaving the house. By walking into the park. By stepping into the library. By greeting strangers. By choosing not to remain invisible.

Forty years after she first "planted" herself in Rosewood Park, Yvonne Sandoval still moves through the city as if it were an extended home. She is at the library, the Senior Center, Camp Commerce, and she is in conversation with strangers who quickly become friends.

If you ask her for directions, she will give them. If you sit quietly long enough, she will notice. If you enter a room uncertain, she will be the one to break the tension with a greeting that insists you belong.

Cities are often measured in budgets, buildings, and boundaries. But their true endurance rests elsewhere—in the people who decide, year after year, to invest their time in others. In Commerce, Yvonne is one of those people who has spent four decades making sure the doors are always open.

Turbo Boost to the 80s!

Alex Rendon

Turbo Boost to the 80s!

Alex Rendon has been living in the City of Commerce since he was just one-day old. While he's moved around within the city, Commerce has always been home. What makes it feel like home are all his great memories.

One particularly exciting memory is when he was able to see the filming of a Season 2 episode of the popular television series, Knight Rider. The series focused on the partnership of a former police officer and an AI-boosted car called KITT. Every week they worked together to fight injustice. This particular episode featured the Citadel of old, and an especially dangerous adversary-an armored semi-truck called Goliath. In order to film, they had cars double-parked on Atlantic Boulevard and took over the gas station. Alex got to see KITT and even a controlled fire that was part of the show. It was an exciting scene for a child to witness!

Alex remembers many fun activities. In addition to 5K runs, such as the Turkey Trot, there were also bike competitions! Cinco de Mayo was a big celebration and you could see lots of Low Riders. There were also trips to see the USS Midway, an aircraft carrier that was decommissioned in 1992 and now serves as a museum and memorial in San Diego.

Daily life in Commerce was also different. The park had two pool tables, arcade machines, and lots of other games. There was also a movie room, with high-intensity speakers. It made for an unforgettable movie experience. Sometimes the movies were scary, which he thought was important because it helped them to learn how to deal with scary things. And who could forget the trips to Camp Commerce? In addition to the parks, transportation was easy, with all the bus routes. Besides lots of books, the libraries had arts and crafts and switched from electric typewriters to computers.

Alex saw the Citadel transformed from a tire factory to a mall back in the 1990s. He has fond memories of a hotel near Washington and Telegraph, where he and his cousin would DJ. They would also visit the rooftop and enjoy the view of the city.

To those living in Commerce, or considering moving here, Alex recommends taking advantage of all the great opportunities here, whether in transportation, libraries, parks, or children's sports. Two special opportunities for young adults are the Miss Commerce Pageant and the Young Man of the Year. Some children (and their parents) dream of participating in these events. More than that, he advocates volunteering and getting involved with charities. You can serve your community and create great memories.

Growing Up in the City of Commerce

Marlem Madrigal

Growing Up in the City of Commerce

I have had the privilege of calling the City of Commerce home for thirty-six years. Growing up here wasn't just about living in a city—it was about becoming part of a community. Commerce, with its deep sense of belonging and commitment to its residents, provided me with countless opportunities. From youth sports leagues and arts and crafts classes to the invaluable resources at the public library, Commerce offered everything I needed not only to grow up but also to thrive.

One of my earliest childhood memories is walking into the City of Commerce Public Library. It wasn't just a place with books—it was a gateway to adventure, learning, and a connection to the world. I would spend hours in the children's section, surrounded by books on all topics imaginable, feeling like I could escape to any place or time. More than just books, the library offered programs that allowed me to socialize and explore my interests, whether it was through a summer reading challenge or the arts and crafts workshops they hosted. Little did I know those hours spent at the library would set the foundation for the work I would do for the city later on in life.

The City of Commerce is unique in how it invests in its residents, especially its youth. The various activities available, from cooking classes to traveling sports teams, created an environment where young people like me could thrive. My family did not have a lot of money, but the opportunities provided by the city made sure I had access to experiences that were enriching and fulfilling. I remember playing on the city's recreational softball team, a program funded by the city's recreation department, and traveling to other parks in the city with my friends, creating lifelong memories. These experiences helped me build confidence and develop a love for teamwork that would follow me through the years.

As a teenager, I joined the City of Commerce's Youth Employment (YES) program. This program was a turning point in my life, providing me with my first job and the chance to contribute to my community in a meaningful way. Through YES, I began working for the city's parks and recreation department. It wasn't just about getting paid; it was about being part of something larger than myself.

I learned work ethic, responsibility, and the importance of serving others. The YES program opened doors for me, teaching me valuable skills and helping me realize my passion for public service.

Fast forward a few years, and I found myself working for the City of Commerce in a role that would become my career: serving in libraries. I can still remember my first days working at the library, stepping into the very place that had been so crucial to my growth as a child. Although I no longer work for the City of Commerce, I still get to help others find the same joy and learning that I did in those early years. Working in the library allowed me to see first-hand the power of resources and programs that can change lives. It's not just about checking out books—it's about offering a space for connection, learning, and personal growth.

Looking back, I can see just how much the City of Commerce has shaped me. The programs available to me as a child weren't just recreational—they were transformative. Whether it was through the sports leagues, art classes, or library programs, each experience helped mold me into the person I am today. And now, as I give back to the community through my work, I see how the same opportunities I had continue to impact the lives of young people in Commerce. I'm proud to say that I'm part of a legacy—a city that believes in its residents and is committed to providing opportunities for growth.

The City of Commerce has been more than just a place I grew up in; it has been a part of my journey, my growth, and my success. From the YES program to working in the library, the city's support has shaped me, and I'm thankful for every moment spent here. As I continue to serve my community, I am reminded of the powerful impact a city can have on its residents, and how the programs that seem so simple can change lives in profound ways.

Family Legacy in the City

Elsie Cardoza

Family Legacy in the City

I'm a longtime resident of Commerce and have been here since before the city was incorporated. I still live here and even work for the city. We call ourselves homegrown because we are proud of our city and all it has to offer children, seniors, and residents.

My first memory of Commerce is the reading club. Back then, it was called the Busy Bee. We were in it for over five-maybe even 10 years. It was a really good program. We loved it! I also became involved in sports, such as baseball and basketball.

At the time, there were only two libraries: Atlantic and Rosewood. Later, libraries were added to the Veterans and Bristow neighborhoods. Then the city offered free buses. Everybody got around town that way, if we weren't riding our bikes, that is. We would jump on the bus and we'd go all over.

As I got older, I had my family, and I got my children involved in all the programs also. They graduated from preschool, played baseball, and basketball. My daughter was a cheerleader and joined tap and ballet. Now that she's older, she's raising my grandkids here. They've been involved in baseball, soccer, and basketball and went on to play high school sports. It's become a tradition.

The culture here has mostly been Mexican, but there are other minorities, too. It's a very friendly city. Everybody is like family. Everybody knows each other. When I was in school, if I did something wrong, I knew someone was going to tell my mother. You couldn't get away with anything in Commerce. You know, *anything*.

But don't let that scare you. Commerce is a welcoming community and beautiful place to live and raise a family. Come and join us-- join the family. To our younger residents, I'd like to say, please get involved with the city. Take advantage of its programs, including scholarships for residents. Have confidence in yourself and stay focused on the road ahead.

I began working for the city in 1986 and became the Chief Range Master at the Veterans Park shooting range. We trained police officers and community members to shoot. We had a rifle team for our kids and won a lot of championships. Some went on to compete in the Olympics and stuff.

When the range closed, I was transferred to the Senior Center. In total, I've worked for the city for about 40 years. I've been asked about the difference between working at the shooting range and working at the Senior Center. "The guns are safer!" :-P

Rooted in Commerce, Soaring Beyond
Jannine Mancilla

Rooted in Commerce, Soaring Beyond

Some stories begin far from home, but Jannine Mancilla's begins in the city that watched her grow: Commerce—a place that gave her roots and taught her to fly. Commerce is not merely a backdrop to her life; it is a living presence that shaped every step of her journey. Her first birthday was celebrated here, but that is only a small part of a much larger story. Commerce watched her grow, guided her, and quietly shaped the person she would become.

As a child, she moved through the city as if it were an extension of herself—running between parks with her siblings, climbing, laughing, learning to swim, and joining team after team. She discovered what it meant to belong to a place that noticed her, where familiar faces greeted her at every turn. Every detail, no matter how small, is etched into memory: the original park before it moved, the trailer that served as the Parks and Recreation office, the old pool where the library now rises, and always, the snack bar—the chili cheese fries, in particular, a flavor she would always associate with those memories.

Her parents, immigrants from Mexico, chose Commerce deliberately. They sought more than a house or a yard, they wanted a place where their children could flourish. Commerce responded with quiet generosity: parks, libraries, programs, mentors, and neighbors who watched over children without being asked. It offered structure, opportunity, and room to explore.

And then there was the library—the heart of her world.

Her mother began as a volunteer, later became a library page, and Jannine naturally followed her into that world. Among shelves and storytimes, she discovered not only books, but also a sense of belonging. She remembers exactly where the poetry books were tucked, the tiny stool she perched on, and a place that made curiosity and learning feel safe to explore. That library became a constant thread—first as a child, then as a volunteer, and finally as staff. It was a place where she witnessed leadership lived rather than spoken: women like Beatriz Sarmiento, Annabelle Palacios, Susana Rosales, and Stacy Sánchez showed her, day after day, that power and compassion could coexist.

Commerce inspired her to be courageous. Sports taught her to take up space: softball, volleyball, basketball, and even a brief and clumsy season of soccer nudged her forward. The Miss Commerce pageant taught her to speak, to present herself, and to claim her voice. The first time she competed, she didn't win—but she walked away proud simply for trying. The second time, older, steadier, supported by mentors who believed in her, she was crowned Miss Fourth of July 2012. Not merely a title, but a quiet confirmation that she had grown, and the city had noticed.

As adulthood unfolded, so did her awareness of the world beyond Commerce. Environmental science sharpened her awareness of the hidden costs of waste and excess. While working at the library, she applied for the Commerce Connect Create grant and launched a clothing swap with her colleague, Enri. That spark became Radical Clothes Swap, a nonprofit that now serves communities across Los Angeles—offering free clothing, keeping garments out of landfills, and reframing fashion as shared rather than disposable. Its values—community, resourcefulness, generosity—are unmistakably Commerce-born.

Through it all, Jannine has become, in spirit, an elder sibling: a mentor, a guide, and a witness to the growth of a new generation. She recalls places that no longer exist—the donut shop by Lucky Guys, the VHS rental store where owners reserved films for her family, and Herman's yellow snack cart, which kept a ledger for children who couldn't pay immediately. Commerce is small, yes, but its power lies in connection: neighbors who see you, care for you, and weave a safety net of attention, pride, and love.

When asked what makes her proudest, she speaks first of her parents, then the city that nurtured them. Commerce offered what time and money could not: opportunity, guidance, and a community that taught her who she could be. She has never lived elsewhere. She has grown alongside this city, watching herself and Commerce transform together, and watching new generations step into the spaces that once shaped her.

Commerce is more than where she comes from. It is where Jannine Mancilla learned who she could be.

A Queen to Remember
Elizabeth Rodarte

A Queen to Remember: Elizabeth Rodarte

Elizabeth's journey in Commerce begins with childhood memories that linger for a lifetime. Some of her clearest and happiest moments come from Bandini Park, where she attended the early childhood program. She still remembers her teacher, Miss Loretta, and the way she made the classroom feel warm and safe, like a second home. For Elizabeth, going to school was never a burden. It was something that brought her joy. It was a place where she felt welcomed.

There are small details that remain vivid in her memory. Snack time, for example. The plain cookies and sweet juice felt like a treat. It wasn't just food, it was a moment to share, to laugh, and to feel like part of the group. Those simple moments are what sparked her love for school and for community.

Elizabeth saw how Commerce changed over time, how it shifted from being mostly industrial to a community that sought to better support its people. As the city moved forward, she was also finding her own path.

Sports were a very important stage of her life. Being part of the City of Commerce women's water polo team taught her discipline, commitment, and teamwork. It wasn't easy. There were long practices, exhaustion, and difficult moments, but also lessons that stayed with her forever. Everything she experienced in the pool later helped her in school and in her adult life.

When Elizabeth thinks of Commerce, the first thing she remembers is its people. The city was filled with hardworking families, supportive neighbors, and a strong sense of community pride. It was a place where many people knew each other, where neighbors greeted one another, and offered support. It felt like one big family.

Over the years, the city has changed. It has become more diverse, and some traditions have faded. Elizabeth remembers the Miss Commerce pageant with great fondness. This event meant a lot to many young women, especially Latinas. It wasn't just a competition. It was a space to feel seen, valued, and confident. For her, that experience was transformative and built her confidence at an important stage in her life. She was Miss Commerce in the year 2000. Despite the changes, Elizabeth believes the heart of Commerce is still there. That spirit of community, pride, and resilience can still be felt.

Some of her most cherished memories are tied to the city's traditions: the Fourth of July at Rosewood Park, families sitting on blankets, children running around, laughter, and fireworks lighting up the sky. The parades, sports tournaments, and festivals weren't just events, they were moments that brought people together and strengthened the bonds between neighbors.

The library, the parks, and even the city's public transportation had a significant impact on her life. The library was a place to learn and dream, while the parks were spaces where friendships and leadership was created, and the buses gave her the independence and ability to move around the city. All of this shaped the person she is today.

Commerce gave her much more than programs or activities. It gave her confidence, a sense of belonging, and roots. Elizabeth is proud to be from this community because of its people, its history, and the way families support one another. It may be a small city, but it is full of heart and strength. It is a place where neighbors become family and memories are passed down from one generation to the next.

To Elizabeth, Commerce is a hidden gem--an authentic place, shaped by real stories and lived experiences. It is a place that teaches who you are and where you come from. When she thinks about the future, she hopes that new generations will stay involved, listen to the stories of those who came before them, and protect what makes this community special.

Commerce and the Race that Won it All

Laura Pérez

Commerce and the Race that Won it All

Can you tell us a little bit about yourself?
My name is Laura Pérez; I have been a Parks and Recreation commissioner for about 18 years. I have also been involved with the library, the Teen Center, and the Senior Center. I have attended many city activities, sports, banquets, senior center programs, and teen center programs.

I've been very active with the city's 5K run, the 4th of July event, Cinco de Mayo, Easter Sunday celebrations, and many of the parks and city activities offered. I've been getting more involved with the library and the Senior Center, now that I'm not working. So, I'm coming more to the Senior Center. This morning, we had a meet and greet with the sergeant and the officers. It's always rewarding for me to be able to attend, help, and get involved with the community.

Can you share your earliest memory of living in Commerce?
The earliest memory that I have is when I was selected to be commissioner. I do think that back in the day, a council member was the one who appointed me to be a Parks and Recreation Commissioner, which really changed my life. That really helped me learn more about Commerce and get to know a lot of the residents.

What brought you to Commerce and what was life like when you first arrived?
My parents and I moved to Commerce in 1976, and I have lived in the city ever since. It changed my life because it's a small city. It's a small community and I love that we all know each other.

Can you tell us a story or an experience that you have had in Commerce?
I have experiences every day when I attend different programs. You get to meet different people. It's good to get to know them and have a conversation with them.

How would you describe the people of Commerce when you first moved here? How has the community changed over the years?
When I first moved into Commerce, the community wasn't too

friendly, but over the years, I started getting to know more of my neighbors. That's when I got involved as a Parks and Recreation Commissioner. You have that community sense that you get to know your neighbors, and it's always good to know who they are in case you need anything. It also helps them feel comfortable coming to you if they need anything.

What traditions or events from the past do you remember from Commerce?
I'm going to say the one that I do remember. Two years ago, the Senior Center put on a prom night, and it was very nice to see all the seniors dressed in their evening gowns and tuxedos. It was nice because a lot of them didn't have the opportunity to go to their own proms. We had a king and a queen. It was a community effort between 16 different cities, and it was hosted at the Commerce Casino, and to me, that was amazing! Many seniors didn't have the opportunity to go to their high school prom, but now they could experience it.

What role did the city's libraries, parks, or buses play in shaping your experiences in the community?
The library really helped my kids with school programs. They were always there getting books, getting information, and help because I'm not good at math. It's good to get our kids involved in the library, because they offer many resources.

What are some of the most significant changes you've witnessed in Commerce throughout the years?
I believe a lot has changed in the City of Commerce. COVID changed everyone's life for the worse, but luckily, we've been recovering and things are getting back to normal. Being involved with the City of Commerce and the different activities helps us feel like we're moving forward.

Were there any landmarks or businesses that are no longer around that you miss?
Yes. The Hyatt Hotel was located on the corner of Washington and Telegraph. It was an outstanding hotel that was here in the City of Commerce for years. Unfortunately, it had to close its doors and with time it was demolished. Now, it's a brand-new building, but it was an outstanding hotel back in the day.

How has being a part of the City of Commerce impacted your life?
It has impacted my life because I was a Parks and Rec Commissioner. It did help me meet a lot of people, help the community, get to know more about the City of Commerce, not only with the Parks and Rec, but with the different departments.

What makes you most proud to be from Commerce?
All the benefits that the City of Commerce offers its residents. No other city has what we have. I'm grateful that we have all of those benefits and we can take advantage, especially when you have children because they can be part of the water polo, the swim team or the dance team. The city offers so many different sports and activities for our children.

If you have to describe Commerce to someone who has never been here, what would you say? Commerce is great to their residents and the entire family. You have to move into Commerce.

How would you like future generations to remember Commerce?
I would encourage them to first get to know the history of Commerce, see where Commerce came from when it wasn't yet an incorporated city, and just learn and keep the tradition that Commerce offers to the residents.

What advice would you give to younger, new residents of Commerce about preserving the city's history and community spirit?
Get involved and get to know your city and get to know your city officials. Learn as much as you can and be proud of living in the City of Commerce.

Is there anything else you would like to add?
I would like to thank the City of Commerce for all that it offers residents. Back in 1995, my mother had an aneurysm. We almost lost her, but thanks to the City of Commerce offering the 5K and all the exercise classes that my mom used to take back in the day, that really helped her come out of her depression, she was very depressed during her illness. That helped her to rehabilitate. She's

been doing that 5K since 1995 and up to last year. She's very proud of all the medals and trophies that she earned during the 5K. So, I'm very thankful to the City of Commerce for offering that.

My Commerce Story and Adventures
Helen Gonzales

My Commerce Story and Adventures

Can you tell us a little bit about yourself?
I was a journalism major and have a B.A. from California State University, Los Angeles. I've been living in Commerce (Veterans area) since 2007. I love writing. I feel like it's my therapy. Sometimes I wake up in the night and write. I love history. I'm a mom with adult children who grew up in East Los Angeles and Commerce. I'm also a mask collector. I went to a Craft and Folk Art Museum Mask Festival in the Wilshire area that inspired me to collect masks because it made me see a common thread amongst people. The unity of people made me feel good. I could see how we all use masks in different ways. Another big joy in my life is the Renaissance Faire. I started going in 1994 because when I was in college, studying Shakespeare, I was questioning what was the big deal about him.

How long have you lived in Commerce?
I've been living in Commerce (Veterans Area) since 2007.

Has Commerce changed since you first started living here?
During the pandemic, the city strived to celebrate events, such as Halloween. They had a Drive-in at Veterans Park and a Drive-thru Halloween night. They even gave us a backpack with different things, including a book about Commerce.

What are some of your first memories of Commerce?
When I was a kid in the 60's, my older sister and I used to ride the bus to Rosewood Park so we could swim in the indoor pool. It was the only pool in the area that was indoors and I thought that was so cool. We had a big family and my dad would say, "If you are going to go, take your little sister." It wasn't the Brenda Villa pool. This pool was closer to where City Hall is today.

Another memory is when another sister used to live across the street from where the "Village" is today. The "Village" was not there at that time. There was a place called The Great Western Exhibit Center. Sometimes they had Pow-Wows, but I always wanted to get on the Big Slide they had. I might have been too little, I think. Another memory of the City of Commerce and my most cherished, is Camp Commerce. I've never heard of any other city having a camp for their residents. I felt very spoiled going to Camp Commerce. We would go on a bus to Lake Arrowhead and find our cabins. Then we were served breakfast, lunch and dinner. They also had crafts, a swimming pool and a lounge where we would watch movies and play pool. Then they would drive us around to different locations for shopping, hiking or canoeing. This was a weekend of fun, for just $15 dollars.

When I was visiting my old neighborhood, I ran into an old neighbor and she asked where I was living. I told her Commerce. She said, "Ohhh! Commerce? I always wanted to live there because I heard they always do such nice things for the residents." Maybe you'll join us one day.

The City of Commerce
and the Importance of Five Minutes

Artemio Navarro

The City of Commerce and the Importance of Five Minutes

Could you tell us a little bit about yourself?
My name is Artemio Navarro and I'm a resident of the City of Commerce. I first moved here in 1976. Over the years, I have been an active member of this community. I served as president of the Lions Club and president of the Holy Name Society. I was on the board of directors for the Sister City and part of the Democratic Club. I've also had the honor of serving as a City of Commerce council member and mayor.

Would you share a little bit about one of those organizations?
East L.A. Jaycees is an organization that was formed to help young men become community members. In 1986-1987, I was president of the East Los Angeles Jaycees. Being president of the organization made me the chairman of the East Los Angeles Christmas Parade that occurred every Sunday after Thanksgiving. This was a way of getting the community involved with our East L.A. area. Of course I also thought of the City of Commerce! I contacted Dr. Guerra, who was mayor at the time, and invited him and the City Council to participate in the East Los Angeles Christmas Parade.

Dr. Guerra invited me for lunch at Steven's Steakhouse the following day. I went to Steven's at our appointed time, and the owners, Virginia and Jim Filipan, sat us at the mayor's table. I didn't know the mayor had a table! On his arrival, Dr. Guerra asked me several questions, including, where my family is from.

I told him that my dad is from Aguascalientes, but immigrated to the United States as a young boy. Mexican revolutionary leader, Pancho Villa, had gone to Aguascalientes after losing a terrible battle; he lost so many men that he went to recuperate and draft young boys to join his army. My grandfather was very cautious and put everybody on the train that night, including my father, and his brothers and sisters. They immigrated to El Paso, Texas. From El Paso, they came to Boyle Heights and eventually bought a home and raised a family. It turns out that Dr. Guerra is also from Aguascalientes, and he is the founder of the Sister City Group between Commerce and Aguascalientes. My story must have impressed him because he asked me to become a commissioner. I was appointed as a traffic commissioner through Dr. Guerra, and I got to meet several council members. One council member in particular was Sheriff Jim Dimas. I met Jim and Barbara Dimas, and we hit it off. My wife Sally and I became close friends with them.

During that period in time, there was a possible vacancy in the city council, and they had asked me if I would consider running. I didn't think much of it at the time, but Jim Dimas, and council members Dr. Guerra, and Ruth Adalco all encouraged me to run for city council.

After much thought and discussions with my wife, I decided to go ahead. Jim Dimas helped my campaign by introducing me to several Commerce city founders, including Mrs. Bristow, Alex Ortiz, and Ruben Batres, who was also running. Ruben and I became very close friends because we shared a vision for the city's future. We both ran and asked of our residents, "After you vote for me, make sure your second vote goes for Ruben," and vice versa. Fortunately for Ruben and me, in 1988 we were both elected to the city council.

During that period of time, they had just hired a new city manager named Lou Shepherd. Prior to this, he had worked as a redevelopment director in Pasadena. So Lou Shepherd, Ruben Batres, and I were newcomers to the City of Commerce. From that point on, we were in constant contact, thinking about what to do with the Uniroyal Building (where tires had been made). I have pictures of that vacant lot with big walls. Eventually that building would become the Citadel Outlets!

Can you talk about your earliest memory of living in Commerce?
I moved to Commerce in 1976. I was a teacher at Eastmont Elementary School and lived right across the street from the Great Western. I was fascinated by all the programs the city had. At that time, I didn't know anything about Camp Commerce, but was interested in youth and the programs the city had for our children. I was very proud of Commerce, spending the time and resources to help our youth become great citizens.

I was also interested in the library. At that time, I was working on my MA degree and needed a place to study. So the library became my friend. I was constantly there and there was even a time when the library was open on Sundays. I would go, concentrate on writing my term paper or my thesis, and get my projects completed. This was way before computers, so you needed an encyclopedia to help with your research. Thank goodness the library was open!

I was very instrumental in having the Atlantic Library built. When I was mayor, I focused on getting the library built for the residents of the Bandini neighborhood. I pushed the council members, since we had promised those residents a library and I never let them forget it. So eventually the Bandini (Atlantic) Library was built; it was a place where kids from that neighborhood could come, get tutoring, and do their homework.

Could you tell a story or a share an experience that you've had in Commerce?
One day when I was campaigning in the Veterans Park neighborhood, a resident shared how grateful she was that we have Camp Commerce. She couldn't afford to take her two boys on vacations, but Camp Commerce allowed even those with modest budgets to have a week-long vacation away from home. When you take a trip and have Lake Arrowhead in your backyard, with mountain air, arts and crafts, hikes, and a swimming pool, it's going to be a great time! The most memorable part about it for me was having camp counselor Ruben Villalobos entertain with camp stories. So, if you're not aware of Camp Commerce, go check it out!

How would you describe the people of Commerce when you first moved here? And how has the community changed over the years?
I was fortunate to have met so many good people in Commerce. The founders of our city had a vision that even today, I hope the city council respects. People like the city founders, Mrs. Bristow, Mr. & Mrs. Maese, and Valentina Bassett saw Commerce as a place where people could raise their kids and live a good life. We are a model city and people have copied us.

We are fortunate to attract businesses. I was here when the Commerce Casino was being built. I was here when the Citadel was being built. I was holding scissors when we did the grand opening for the Citadel and Mr. Trammell Crow, who oversaw the development of the Citadel, was playing with my two little girls. I have fraternal twins and he was so entertaining to them that I was surprised that this multi-billionaire fella had time to spend with two little girls who were toddlers at the groundbreaking ceremony of the Citadel.

Being in Commerce has been a gratifying experience for me. I love the city. I happened to be the mayor at the time we were attempting to build the mix master. We were once number 260 on the California to-do list. That particular year, I traveled to Sacramento sixteen times to help make it happen. I spoke to Bill Lockyer who was the Speaker Pro Tem, Assemblyman Javier Becerra, lobbyists, and Caltrans heads. With continued efforts, we were able to move up the list to number 160 and then number 60. When we reached number eight, Los Angeles County Supervisor Gloria Molina brought in a million dollars, the railroad provided a million dollars, and we had the funding to proceed with the mix master.

That's what it takes. You have to have the determination and the willpower to go up there and make sure they know who you are when they see you and they know what you want because eventually they'll grant you your wish.

What traditions or events from the past do you remember fondly?
I'm grateful to have participated in our celebrations of the Fourth of July and Veterans Day. In fact, I have a keepsake from Veterans Day. At that time, Congresswoman Lucille Roybal was our representative in Washington. During our celebration at Veterans Park, she gave me a flag that was folded into a triangle. She told me it had flown over the Capitol. It's preserved in a special case and remains a treasured piece of history.

What are some of the most significant changes you've witnessed in Commerce throughout the years?
When I first moved into Commerce, the village was the first thing I noticed. Living across the street from the village, I was kind of heartbroken to see the Great Western get torn down. Through

the influence of Senator Art Torres, we were able to get that land from the state and build the village. In acknowledgment to Senator Torres, the city council at the time wanted to name a street after him. Art was very gracious to deny or decline the offer. He did say, "If you want to name a street after me, I'd rather have you name it after my grandfather." His grandfather's name is Joaquin. So in the village, there is a street called Joaquin Court named after Art Torres' grandfather because he didn't want it named after himself, but he did want to acknowledge the contributions his grandfather had made for him as he was growing up. Now we have the Veterans Park neighborhood that's grown. I remember when they were building the development on Pacific Drive. I remember when the Montebello School Board fought the City of Commerce over what was then called the Gage Drive-In. That became a school for the Montebello Unified School District. It was very sad that that school did not survive because that was a beautiful corner for a school. Trammell Crow wanted to build warehouses and provide jobs for the residents, but the school board used eminent domain, a program to take property away from cities to build that school. Unfortunately, over time, there were not enough students to guarantee the funding for that school. We didn't have enough students to fill it. So that school did close down.

How has being a part of the City of Commerce impacted your life?
I made a decision to move here and raise a family. I have four children and have been married to my wife Sally for over 40 years. We've been involved with so many events here in the city, both in an official capacity, and as parents. We raised our kids here and saw the great things that have been done for our children. The school programs here in Commerce bend backwards for our children. I was very fortunate to see great principals come to our schools and help coordinate the teaching and education of our children. I've grown with the city. My married life and political life have been with the city. My friends are here with the city. I've been honored to be friends with some of the founders of our city and appreciate the great people that have lived in Commerce, especially the ones who helped me in my campaign. I have lots of great memories.

What makes you most proud to be from Commerce?

Being a resident is number one. I have never failed to vote in our city. In fact, I have been hospitalized with COVID and voted absentee. It's such an important decision to make when we vote for our elected officials that I have never, ever failed to vote.

The city itself has done so much for its residents. It speaks for itself and has become a landmark city for many in California. When we would go to conferences, if we mentioned to other council members that we're from Commerce, their eyes would light up. They were aware of the programs Commerce was doing. We are fortunate to have funding that comes from the Citadel, the Commerce Casino, and our industrial base, so that we can provide for our residents. People in Commerce sometimes don't realize how lucky we are because we take it for granted. Other communities don't have the same resources we do, including our swimming pool and gymnasiums. We were the first city in California to build an indoor pool. In 1960, when the first Aquatorium was built, it cost a million dollars. That was unheard of in 1960, plus being indoors. Nobody had that in California. Now we have our second indoor pool. We are so glad that our residents can benefit from all of these opportunities. I hope we can continue these programs for our kids because they pay off.

If you had to describe Commerce to someone who has never been here, what would you say?
You'd be surprised with the opportunities residents have in Commerce and the facilities we have, including our gym and the Brenda Villa Aquatic Center, which is the envy of many cities. We have such beautiful neighborhoods. Street sweeping occurs every week and we have good trash haulers who pick up our waste to keep our city clean. I used to be the chairman of the Anti-Gang Task Force. We made great strides, partnering with the sheriff to prevent gang members from recruiting our Commerce kids. The council passed many ordinances to keep gang members abate, so our Commerce kids would not be involved with them. We started the YES program, a program that gave youth summer jobs, enough money that they could afford a prom or even afford tuition, books, and school supplies. The YES program was a great program for our kids to benefit from, and it gave them an opportunity to see how the city works. Sometimes some of those YES workers would go on to work for the city.

How would you like future generations to remember Commerce?

Not to forget the past. I want them to remember the vision of our founders. They envisioned a city where kids can grow up, become model citizens, and where the city can provide our residents with opportunities in employment, education, and events that would help them be proud of where they come from. Opportunities for our residents are budgeted and not many cities can afford what we've been able to do. So I want our residents to be aware of the sacrifices that were made in the past, and how they could keep Commerce going. We have to keep our city clean. We have to keep our city free of crime. One thing that gives people an idea of what your city is like is when they drive up and down the streets and they see how residents take care of their homes. That alone tells outsiders, "This is Commerce. This is a reflection of our city."

What advice would you give to younger or new residents of Commerce about preserving the city's history and community spirit?

Educate yourself. Learn about your city's history. We wrote a book in 1989 about the history of our City of Commerce (City of Commerce: An Enterprising Heritage). Ruth Adalco, who was the mayor at the time, helped fund the book so that residents could go to the library and read the book. One was given to every household so that they could read about the history of the City of Commerce. We have a very proud history.

There is a story of Dean Mericle, an ex-Navy radio man during World War II and member of the [Commerce] Citizens' Committee for Incorporation. In 1959, Lakewood had decided to incorporate and become their own city. At that time, our founders thought, "Why don't *we* become a city, too?" At the same time, Downey was thinking of annexing the City of Commerce. Our businesses, our tax base, is what attracted them.

By five minutes, Dean Mericle was able to go up the elevator and present our petition for cityhood to the Board of Supervisors. In those five minutes, he beat the City of Downey, who wanted to annex the city. Because of Dean Mericle, those five minutes of him getting to the Board of Supervisors first, and presenting them with the petition, the paperwork, and the filings that were needed, the City of Commerce was born. Otherwise, it would have been the City of Downey. I think residents can benefit from learning this part of the city's history. Five minutes, that's how much time it took.

The Teacher Who Lit Up the City
Carmen Márquez Cooper

The Teacher Who Lit Up the City

Can you tell us your name and a little bit about yourself?
My name is Carmen Márquez and I've lived in the city about 40 years (I'm going to be 77 years old). I'm so happy! I was a teacher and a counselor for 40 years with the Montebello Unified School District. During the same time, I was on the Education Commission or the Library Commission, where I learned a lot about the city. We came to see the library as the heart of the city. I've talked to many people and they don't have the services that are offered here in Commerce. We've got many experts sharing a lot of information and that's been really fantastic.

Can you share your earliest memory or memories from living in Commerce?
We used to live in City Terrace, where there were a lot of gangs. We moved to Commerce for safety. My cousins, the Davaloses, were already here. They loved all the activities that were offered and it was safe to walk. You could go out at nine o'clock at night and there was not a problem.

I was 13 years old when we moved. The city had the beautiful pool [Aquatorium], so we had swimming lessons and joined the swim team. It was fantastic. Really different. We could walk to the pool without worrying about locking our doors. And in case you're wondering, bread was 25 cents and gas was 25 cents!

One of the wonderful things we had was the 72 Club at Bell Gardens High School. It was a swimming club, run by the water polo coach. You had to swim 72 laps, which is a mile. Every year lifeguards from Commerce would be our chaperones and we'd go to the Colorado River in a big bus. We went on canoe rides in the river for a whole week! It was fantastic! It was great energy. We learned a lot.

On those occasions when we'd go out, my parents would say, "No, don't mess up because by the time you get home, I'm gonna know what you did." Everybody knew each other and would take care of each other.

Tell us a story or an experience that you have had in Commerce. It could be something memorable or something that comes to your head.

We were from the era of the Cold War. There was a lot of stress, because we worried about what would happen if a bomb was dropped. If you were a girl in high school, you had to kneel down in your skirt and touch the floor.

On Fridays, everybody (Bell Gardens and Commerce) would go to the high school football games. At that time, Commerce kids were being taught football, but coaches from the Gardens weren't really giving them a chance to play. Perhaps not surprisingly, Bell Gardens developed a reputation for losing. Things finally began to change and they had a winning team. Why? Because they let our Commerce kids play!

How would you describe the people of Commerce when you first moved here and how has the community changed over the years?

Every single school in Montebello had an English language learner classroom for parents. At that time, the expectation was that everyone would learn English and there was a big push to make it happen. A lot of people who spoke Spanish worried about being welcome. Today there's hardly any English language development or ESL located at school sites. The City of Commerce Library's Literacy Center does offer some help with English language development. The program is called Cafecito, and allows people to enjoy coffee while practicing their English. It's a very safe and inviting atmosphere that empowers our people to learn English.

It's very important that we keep our first language and know our culture—our roots. I went to East Los Angeles College and California State University, Los Angeles, and never felt we were Chicanas. We didn't fit here and we didn't fit in Mexico. Where do we fit? Where do I fit? Once I figured that out, it was like cool... You have a beautiful culture. We need to know our culture. We need to know where we come from and all the fantastic and beautiful things that our culture offers. An invaluable place to see this is the library. Just think of all the fantastic programs the library offers—and for all ages. There are programs for children, teens, and adults. We need to get that word out! I absolutely love Read Across America. There are author visits and book clubs. For "NASA Night," we have scientists and engineers giving talks, while the Old Town Sidewalk Astronomers bring their telescopes to look up into the sky. Kids get to identify planets and stars and that's so cool! Not a lot of cities have that. Day of the dead is really important because a lot of people don't understand what that is. As Latinos, life and death are really connected. We need to know about each one. Through it all, we're reminded of this beautiful part of our culture that we should be practicing every day.

What role did the city's libraries, parks and buses play in shaping your experiences in the community?
My granddaughter is pretty high functioning on the autistic spectrum. Parks and Recreation guided her and helped her run for the Miss Commerce Contest. She had such a wonderful experience. We worked hard with her and she got up and spoke in front of all these people. She still remembers it. She tells people it's on YouTube. Look at my picture. It really... brings tears to my eyes. Everybody was so inclusive. Everybody fit here, too. We're like a big family. Sometimes a little dysfunctional, but we're family. We're real here and full of love.

What's it like being on the Library Commission?
I recommend it highly. You find out what's really happening. You get to know people and see what's going on in the back. Everybody's so hardworking. It's a great connection! It's also our opportunity to go out in our community to spread the word. I would go to schools, such as Suva Intermediate. I used to teach and counsel at Suva, so I'd speak to that principal. We would also take flyers over. The library was very supportive! Please seek to join a commission or attend commission meetings. Please go to council meetings.

What are some of the most significant changes that you witnessed in Commerce throughout the years?
This beautiful, fantastic, well-planned library setting! You come here, you're welcomed, and you're asked if you need help. It's hard to describe the many activities. Adults can come and do crafts. You can read, and check out movies and music CDs. They sometimes come in multiple languages or big fonts. You can have the whole library in your pocket, and in your phone. Hoopla allows

you to access e-books, e-audiobooks, and more. It's just wonderful! I always encourage kids, especially intermediate and high school students, to take advantage of free online tutoring. All you need is your library card! I think a lot of kids take advantage of it.

Well, talking about business, were there any landmarks or businesses that are no longer around that you miss?
Oh, I miss that 10-story building. In its absence, the freeway and the trains seem louder than ever. Directions are not quite as easy to give… I used to say, "Go to the 10-story building and I'm a block away." I can't do that anymore. I miss Lucky's and Thrifty's. Right now, you know what I miss most? The snack bar. I miss the snack bar! You could go to the pool and then treat yourself to a Fudgsicle!

How has being part of the City of Commerce impacted your life?
There's been so much history here. I taught at Vail High School, the best kept secret in the world. Loved it! That's where I learned about the brick. Bricks were made there and back then, the people who were making them lived in that area. I didn't realize that there was also an airstrip there. "Oh, oh, oh, and did you know that at one time Downey was trying to take over Commerce?" There was a big "barrio." Fortunately, the people who helped incorporate the City moved really fast. They submitted the required paperwork before Downey did and here we are, with a beautiful model city.

What makes you proud of Commerce?
I feel safe here. I lived in Downey for "32 seconds." There were more activities here. This is more of a family, "know your neighbor" place. I was in neighborhood watch for a while.

I raised my three girls here. My grandkids play water polo. We swam. They used to have water ballet and diving at the old pool, which I totally love. Now the bigger thing is water polo, and that's fine. My girls swam and they did the dance classes here in the city. I was thinking about all this stuff. This is not only a safe place, but a place where you can raise your kids, where they're learning good habits, learning how to be team members, learning how to reach out, and learn. We're constantly learning. I think we're born and we have gifts in our lives that we can share, but then we're also asking the world, what can we give back?

This is a place where we can live like that soon-to-be butterfly. You're a chrysalis and then you open up to all the resources that we have, like sports. You get to experiment. Do I like soccer? Do I like swimming? Do I like, you know, and this is a good city to experiment, to try and say, you know, I don't like soccer, but I love swimming. I'm going to focus on water polo.

They learn life skills and travel. When we would travel to games, the furthest we went was Arizona. My grandson got to go to Australia! That's a miracle. That's beautiful. He loved it. The kids get to meet kids from other places and learn about other communities. When we travel, we're representing all the seventh graders in the Montebello Unified School District, but also all the seventh graders across the United States of America. We're practicing a lot of these things, which we might not realize, like knowing what language register to use, wherever they're at, noticing what's around you, showing up dressed appropriately, and able to communicate appropriately. Those are skills that you teach them, but you need to practice them every single day. These activities help with that.

If you had to describe Commerce to someone who who's never been here, what would you say?
I'd say this is a great place to live. Then I would talk a little bit about what used to be here and what is now the Citadel Outlets over there. There was the Wild West, which looked like an empty lot, but was the place they'd bring in fairs and other exciting events. There was a drive-in theater on Gage. There has been a lot of change. It's positive, but not perfect. We don't want perfect. We want progress and moving forward and communicating. I think that's really important, communicating, feeling comfortable in what you need to say and knowing how to say it.

You talked a little bit about being a teacher. What do you think is your legacy as a teacher?
I've always wanted to be a teacher, ever since I was in Kinder. I think it's important that we're out there. When we're born, we come with a lot of knowledge and potential. Our job as teachers is to help plant seeds, so those seeds may open up the beauty and knowledge within, so wonderful miracles may happen. I love it

because you work hard and the students work hard and then you see them grow and accomplish good things.

What advice would you give to younger or new residents that move to Commerce about how to preserve or keep the history or the community spirit alive?
I think the first place they need to come to is the library. They can learn about what's going on in the city, become involved, and find direction.

I've had some friends move into the city and have asked them about important places. I've taken them in my car for a special tour of the city, so they could see some of the highlights. I want to make sure that they know this is more than just industry. I would also suggest that people moving in go to City Hall, meet the Mayor and City Council. I recommend that they attend council meetings, get involved in book clubs, and other programs.

Is there anything else that you would like to add?
I love the summer reading programs! I love the literacy program! That's a big one because they also give out scholarships to eligible Commerce residents. I encourage everyone to learn more and apply (it's for adults, too)! These programs from the library and city create more opportunities to grow. It's never too late to learn and grow!

Last Mayor of the Century and
Mayor of the New Millennium

Lilia León

Last Mayor of the Century and Mayor of the New Millennium

Would you please tell us a little bit about yourself?
My name is Lilia, but everyone calls me Lila. I just love being involved in the City of Commerce, with all our beautiful residents -- all 13,000 of them. Sometime around the early 1990s, then-Mayor Robert Cornejo took an interest in me and put me on the Parks and Recreation Commission. It sparked my interest in our civic organizations. I served on and off a variety of different positions, including as the Chairperson of the Education Commission. We started the College Fair, which is still in existence today, and an Essay Contest. Back then, I found that a lot of junior high school students had never written an essay. We wanted to help. The Essay Contest was held in conjunction with a Bookmark Contest, so that we could reach those in kindergarten, too. They would draw a picture with crayons and then tell us about what they drew.

Fast forward to 1998. I was elected to the City Council. Then I served as Mayor Pro Tem, and Mayor. I served from 1999 to 2000, last mayor of the century, and new mayor of the new millennium! I was one of eight women mayors in Southern California, because there weren't a lot of women serving as mayor. I retired in 2017 as an elected official.

My father, Enrique Hernández, was born in 1908. He was so hardworking that even after mandatory retirement, he still wanted to work. So he came to work for the City of Commerce, where he ultimately retired as a maintenance worker at the age of 86. I have his five-year plaque, his 10-year plaque, and his 15-year plaque. He was shy six months of his 20-year plaque. My mother, Teresa, was a seamstress. She could just look at a design and make it. She used to make dresses for then Mayor Quigley's wife because we lived down the street. My brother fought in the Vietnam War and received a Purple Heart.

I could go on and on about all the people who have made a difference here in the City of Commerce. When you think of Commerce, you think of family. Once you live here, you see this through generations. Nobody wants to leave! I grew up here. I bought a home in the Village and raised my son here. When he got married, he chose to live here and bought a home in the gated community at

Vista Del Rio. He raised his daughters, my beautiful little Isabella and Angelina, and at one time they considered moving. The girls said no, they didn't want to move out of Commerce because it was family and they were part of the girl scouts. So generations of families have grown up here in Commerce—four of mine have.

One notable exception is Irma Lopez. After she got married, her family moved out of Commerce. Irma's brother was my brother's best friend. Irma had a daughter, Nikki Ann. She was nine months old when she met my son, who was a year and a half. They reunited at the old aquatorium. Nikki Ann worked in the aquatorium and he'd go there to work out. He asked her out and eventually they got married.

You'll see that with so many families here. Think of a tree and somehow we're all intertwined. Somebody knows somebody that's married to somebody that has a relative in the City of Commerce. We continue to see families wanting to live here.

Would you tell a story or share an experience that you've had in the City of Commerce?
In 1976, we had a parade to celebrate the bicentennial. Participants were asked to represent different eras. My five year-old son chose the future. So my mother, the seamstress, made him an astronaut suit! I still have it! I made a helmet using the deco page process on a balloon and then sprayed it silver, so he could look like a real astronaut. I served as a chaperone, wearing all white and looking out for all of our little astronauts. We went down Atlantic and up Harbor to City Hall. It was very memorable—unless you ask my son. He doesn't remember!

[On a somewhat related note.] There was a company here in Commerce that made parts for the Space Shuttle. Years later I visited but could only go into the conference room. Credentials were required to go in the back because it's treated like top secret.

What traditions or events from the past, do you remember fondly?
The Miss Commerce Pageant. I ran in 1967; everybody in high school would run. It was held in the old pool. We were given watches to commemorate our participation. I still have mine,

which has Miss Commerce on the back. The winner that year was Loretta Monzo. At that time they allowed Bell Gardens students, but after a year in which most of the court was from Bell Gardens, they reconsidered the rules and required that students be Commerce residents.

When I was the mayor, I was asked to crown Miss Commerce. I did, with the assistance of my little granddaughter. She was so enthralled with the pageant that that night, she wrote on my program booklet, "I want to be Miss Commerce 2020." Unfortunately, COVID happened in 2020, so there wasn't a pageant. It may be for the best, though. My son wasn't convinced his daughter should participate. He was nervous for every single girl and said he would never want his little girl to go up there, but it is something that I hope will continue. Little girls aspire to be Queen and for us, it was a thrill to even be in the pageant. You would go down the middle of the runway, down the side and then up the middle of the runway. It was exciting, very exciting! The Queen would serve as an ambassador and go to city events. Little girls would come up to the Queen and want to talk and take pictures with her. Some queens would take it even further, developing some kind of program that they'd like to see come to fruition.

What role did the city's libraries, parks or buses play in shaping your experiences with the community?
I love my library! The library is a world at your fingertips. You can go in and just pick out something and learn so much from a book. It gives you an opportunity to travel and exercise your imagination. When I first got on the council, my vision was to move the Veterans Library to the location of the underground shooting range. I wanted to bring the library down there and add a computer lab, but there were some concerns regarding job loss.

There came a point in my life where I realized that not everybody could read. I thought, oh, my God, not everybody can read. Imagine the impact that could have on their lives. So I volunteered for the library's literacy program. I remember one gentleman who could read, but was having issues with confidence. We started with numbers. I showed him a root word and how if you just put these two letters here and these two letters there, we had a new word. You could see this light pop. After that, he wanted to read everything! So I think that the library is God sent, just God sent. With audio now, you could just sit there and listen to everything. This can be a great alternative for those who have difficulty seeing. Sometimes books are made into movies and that's fine. Movies are not as good as books. The library is fantastic. I'm glad that we have multiple locations, even if small, in the Bandini, Bristow, and Veterans areas.

What are some of the most significant changes you've witnessed in Commerce throughout the years?
The opportunity to interact with the different areas of our city by taking the bus. Those in Bandini are able to go to the Veterans area, Bristow area, or the "Rosini" area, and vice versa. Before it was just little units that would interact with one another.

There's the Commerce Casino—I was there when they did the groundbreaking for the hotel! Then there's the Citadel Outlets. About 20 million people visit the Citadel each year, in this little town of 13,000 people, in which 40,000 to 50,000 people work. I think a lot of people know us because of those two entities. This change has brought traffic, especially during certain times of the year. But if you're innovative, you can get out on Black Friday. You don't have to go under the underpass. Just go down Washington Blvd. to Eastern Blvd. (towards Bell Gardens).

The Scholarship Program is especially noteworthy. Hosted by the City of Commerce Library's Literacy Center (READS), it provides opportunities for many students as they pursue higher education. Thanks to all who have contributed to this program, especially Mr. Haig Papaian, Jr., who was instrumental in supporting and raising the casino's contribution to the program. Everyone who is eligible for the scholarship, meets the requirements, and applies, gets something. So, Commerce residents, apply! Please, please apply. It's always due around mid-April.

How has being a part of the City of Commerce impacted your life?
Being an elected official opened doors, so I could have greater impact on the lives of others. I was invited to join the organization HOPE. It's "HISPANAS ORGANIZED FOR POLITICAL EQUALITY," where Hispanics from Northern California and Southern

California come together to share thoughts and opportunities for elected officials or just women in general. We would gather to see how we could help the next generation, if they wanted to become elected officials, and whether they wanted to change something. It gave me a platform. I was a HOPE graduate of 2000 and learned a lot about political policy and how things work in Sacramento. When I'd go to Sacramento, I could lobby for our city and early money. For example, when there were projects down the I-5, we were able to get money for our Telegraph Road expansion because it connects to the I-5. The more you know, the more you're able to acquire. That I got real quick. Knowledge opened doors and made things more achievable. I think I was born too soon, though. Had I been born about 30 years later, I would have gone beyond local government and made more changes in Sacramento.

I also had the opportunity to join the Jaycees, another volunteer organization. They first allowed women to join in 1986. I became the second woman president. Their motto is Individual Growth Through Community Service. They opened up a world to me: learning how to fundraise, knocking on doors, learning how to speak to strangers, and learning how to do competitions. Service to humanity is the best work of life.

When I became an elected official, I already knew the Brown Act, when to speak, and not to speak. People were packed at a meeting and two started yelling. I hit that gavel and said, no, no, not gonna happen. You come and you have the courtesy to hear what they're gonna say. By the end, everyone spoke and everybody got along. That's what you have to do in politics. You bring everybody together.

What is Camp Commerce?

Camp Commerce is a city owned facility in Lake Arrowhead. Residents have opportunities to visit and enjoy a picturesque getaway. Back in the day, Ruben Villalobos was a counselor and would take us on hikes. One time I remember thinking I can't climb that mountain. He said, "don't look up and don't look back. You look at your two feet in front of you and that's all you concentrate on. Just two feet in front of you. Then before you know it, you're at the top of the mountain." We would all make it.

I still remember that advice to this day. We may face obstacles and think not everything is achievable. For example, if I couldn't find nearby parking or use the valet, I would think, "oh my God, how am I going to walk there?" You get there one step at a time!

My dad loved Camp Commerce. We would go up there with my son. Where else can you go that even comes close? Free transportation. Greatest cooks ever! Plus, you have a meal waiting for you when you arrive. Then breakfast, the next day. Maybe a hike? How about thrift shopping, or taking a walk to Lake Arrowhead? Maybe a movie? It's a great experience for kids, especially those that might not otherwise be able to take a vacation.

If you had to describe Commerce to someone who has never been here, what would you say?
A word that describes this city is serenity. With this life, we think rush, rush, rush, get there, but what's next? Where are we going? In Commerce, we have an opportunity to take a breath on the weekends. You drive through Commerce and there's no traffic, but you can still come to the library and walk around the park. There are still a lot of little places open. I think that's the simplicity of it. You can walk in the park at 11 o'clock at night and feel safe. You see people walking in the evenings, sometimes with their dogs, or families playing. It's serenity-- families want to live in Commerce.

I hope this council finds a way to envision retail with the new generation that maybe isn't ready for a home, but maybe for an apartment. We had been thinking about affordable apartments up and down Washington Blvd. There are also lots of opportunities to find employment here in Commerce. Some people get up and go to work; they don't care about the traffic because it will be gone on the weekends. Whether you're working and living in Commerce, or just living here, you can find serenity.

So how would you like future generations to remember Commerce?
Having a positive attitude every day gives you more longevity. My dad was such a positive and jolly man. I think that's why he lived to 96 and a half. Don't forget that half, you know? He was born in 1908. To future generations, I would suggest you slow down a

little, especially right now. Soon enough you'll have responsibilities and will need to move quickly.

I was born in an era where women went to college to get their MRS degree. What is an MRS degree, you ask? It's a Mrs. Degree. It's to go to college and meet your husband, because women went to college to get married. By the following year, you would have a child. Then you'd stay home as a housewife. That's what I did. I was one of two high school students selected from Bell Gardens High School to attend Los Angeles City College. So, I went to LA City College and that's where I met my husband. He was from Roosevelt. We transferred from LA City College over to East Los Angeles College. After dating for three years, we got married and the following year I had my son, my handsome Richard Leon, who is now 53 years old.

Looking back, I didn't stay married for very long because I found that it wasn't for me. You'll find that a lot of things that seem right, aren't. That's why I think I was born too soon. Should've been born later. I don't know if I would have followed that Mrs. Degree thing. I set my goals and I set a time limit. I wanted to be a homeowner and when the opportunity came, I bought my home at the age of 31 and brought my mom and dad to live with me. Since then, I've gone on to other goals and tried to achieve them. Not everything's achievable, but you try. I think it's Morgan Freeman that asked about the difference between fear and faith. Fear is something that you think is gonna happen and it's bad. Faith is having the opportunity to grow and believing everything is going to be okay. I choose faith all the time. So as long as you have faith, it's gonna be okay; you're gonna go forward.

Be in the moment. Time is gonna go like that. *snaps fingers* Before you know it, you're gonna be 75. Where did the time go? Even my son said, oh my God, [his] oldest is 21. Where'd the time go? My house is 44 years old and he's been in his house for 22 years. So I would tell people to slow down. Enjoy the time you have with the people you care about. You never know how long anyone will be there: family, friends, neighbors, and coworkers.

What advice would you give to younger or newer residents of Commerce about preserving the city's history and community spirit?

Every generation of residents and council members come in with their own vision of how things ought to be. These visions can help or hurt the city. Residents need to know what they're looking for in a representative, because representatives can be nice, or even be your friend. But once they're elected, it's not all black and white. Things don't always go the way you thought they would, but you should strive to preserve what you have. For example, when I was elected in 1998, a resident complained that the street sweeper would go by and leave all the leaves. Our street sweeper had been contracted for over 20 years. I asked why the contract had such a long duration. They said, well, because no one's done anything. I argued that the service should go out to bid every five years. The same person could come back, if the bid is right and they were doing a good job. That's still in effect to this day. So sometimes you have to make change, to preserve the quality of service. Residents need to ensure that their representatives are making the right choices for their city. You, as an individual, as a resident, have the power to say, "Why are they doing that? Why don't we have more staff to help with this?" Employees can "whisper" needs into some resident's ear and then they can whisper to other residents and then change happens. Residents need to look around and if they enjoy what they have, help take steps to preserve it. It comes from your elected officials.

It takes a village of residents to make things happen. Look how we were incorporated. If it wasn't for those individuals that said, "We wanna be an incorporated city," we would be part of Downey.

Commerce: Mi alegría y fortaleza

Martha Moya

Commerce: mi alegría y fortaleza

¿Nos puedes decir cómo te llamas y algo de ti?
Mi nombre es Martha Moya y soy residente de la Ciudad de
Commerce. Nací en Lima, Perú, y vine a la Ciudad de Commerce
en busca de comvivir con otros adultos mayores. Cuando intente
ser parte de los usuarios del *Senior Center* tenía 54 años y no me
aceptaron. Así que tuve que esperar a cumplir los 55 años para
poder ingresar. Desde entonces, sigo aquí.

**¿Puedes compartir un primer recuerdo de vivir en la Ciudad
de Commerce?**
Mi primer recuerdo de vivir aquí fue my positivo, ya que pude
conocer a los miembros de la municipalidad de Commerce, y sobre todo a la señora Oralia Y. Rebollo, quien es muy extrovertida,
le gusta cantar y convivir con todos los adultos mayores.

**¿Qué te trajo a Commerce y cómo era la vida cuando llegaste
por primera vez?**
Cuando llegué a Commerce por primera vez, me gustó mucho la
ciudad, su gente y el ambiente de familiaridad que existe con los
concejales, así como el apoyo que brindan a los residentes. Eso
fue lo que hizo que me quedara. Tras la muerte de mi esposo,
pude haberme mudado, pero no quise. Siempre quiero estar en
Commerce porque aquí me siento en familia.

**Cuéntanos una historia o una experiencia que hayas tenido
en Commerce.**
Aparentemente algunas personas no me aceptaban porque pen-
saban que era más joven. Tal vez sí parecía tener menos edad,
pero no, yo ya tenía 55 años. Al final llegaron a conocerme, con-
vivíamos y todo salió bien.

**¿Cómo describirías a la gente de Commerce cuando te mu-
daste aquí? ¿Y cómo ha cambiado la comunidad a lo largo de
los años?**
Pienso que todos venimos de diferentes culturas, pero tratamos
de adaptarnos. Yo también vengo de otra cultura y me siento
bien aquí. Siento que ya estoy compenetrada en una familia, muy
aparte de la familia que formas en tu hogar.

¿Qué tradiciones o acontecimientos del pasado recuerdas con cariño en Commerce?
Recuerdo celebraciones como el Día de las Madres y la Navidad. También recuerdo el compañerismo, los afectos que nos han dado, tanto como el casino, tarjetas de regalo y la despensa de comida. Esas son algunas cosas bellas que la ciudad nos ha brindado.

¿Qué papel desempeñaron las bibliotecas, los parques o los autobuses de la ciudad en tus experiencias y en la comunidad?
El papel que desempeñaron y hasta ahora que desempeñan es muy bueno, porque eso nos hace sentir que le importamos a la ciudad y que piensan en nosotros y en nuestro bienestar mental.

La biblioteca, por ejemplo, ha sido fundamental. Allí descubrí que me gusta el arte. Estando aquí en la ciudad, he comprobado que todo es diferente y en la biblioteca me siento muy bien. No falto a ninguna de las actividades y cuando falto es porque me olvidé. No me pierdo muchas cosas de Commerce. Vivo en Commerce, respiro en Commerce, como en Commerce, todo en Commerce... ya es mi familia.

¿Veo que vas al Aquatic Center a nadar?
Sí, también voy ahí al *Brenda Villa Aquatic Center*. Pues sí, me gusta nadar y me gusta hacer ejercicios aeróbicos.

¿Cuáles son algunos de los cambios más significativos que has presenciado en Commerce a lo largo de los años?
Los cambios que he presenciado son los del parque. Lo han modificado. Se ve más bello y han puesto bancas para que la gente pueda sentarse. Al menos yo soy una de ellas que me siento, a veces con mi hijo que viene a visitarme y nos sentamos, conversamos y estamos ahí. Después otro cambio también que ha habido es el terreno baldío que está aquí, cerca de transportación. Ese era un terreno baldío en el cual una vez al mes nos llamaban para darnos una despensa y teníamos que hacer una línea ahí. Antes nos daban ropa para escoger. Vendieron el terreno y construyeron apartamentos modernos. Nunca han dejado de darnos la despensa, pero ahora nos la dan frente al *Senior Center*. Ahí hacen la línea para recibir caminando o por vehículo.

Tengo muchos años viniendo a la despensa, desde que prácticamente llegué al *Senior Center*.

¿Había algún lugar emblemático o negocio que ya no existe y qué extrañas?

La Biblioteca Bandini, que se cerró, ahora la están modificando para ponerle más tecnología, computadoras y cuartos de estudio para que los estudiantes tengan más privacidad para poder estudiar. Es una cosa que yo siento le puede ser útil a la comunidad.

¿Cómo ha impactado tu vida ser parte de la Ciudad de Commerce?

Ha tenido un impactado positivo. Me siento bien, apoyada y rodeada de una gran familia. Sobre todo mi salud mental también se ha beneficiado. Hay muchas cosas que te ayudan a ser positivo, a poder seguir en la vida. Hay otras cosas que pasan, que te hacen sentir abatido y caído, pero ahí vamos. A mí la Ciudad de Commerce me da fortaleza.

¿Qué es lo que te hace sentir más orgullosa de ser de Commerce?

Lo que me hace sentir más orgullosa de vivir en Commerce es cuando mi amiga me dice, "Tú vives en la Ciudad de Commerce. Ahí son muy *picky* y la ciudad tiene mucho dinero", pero yo le digo que no es como dicen. Me hace sentir orgullosa porque conozco a los concejales. Puedo ir a hacer un reclamito o puedo pedir ayuda y ya ellos me dicen si sí o no. Sobre todo hay que ser positivos para ver todas las cosas bien positivamente.

¿Si tuvieras que describir a la Ciudad de Commerce a alguien que nunca ha estado aquí, qué le dirías?

Le diría que es una ciudad que tiene mucha ayuda para todos. Hay muchas actividades en la biblioteca y te vas a sentir como en tu casa, así como yo me siento en mi casa.

¿Cómo te gustaría que las futuras generaciones recordaran la Ciudad de Commerce?

Me gustaría que las futuras generaciones la recordaran involucrándose en todos los aspectos que puede haber para los jóvenes, como la natación, los programas de jóvenes en la biblioteca, y que mantenieran el sentido de comunidad y familia.

¿Qué consejo le darías a los residentes más jóvenes o nuevos de Commerce sobre cómo preservar la historia y el espíritu comunitario de la ciudad?
Yo les diría que estudien sobre el inicio de la Ciudad de Commerce, porque Commerce ya cumplió 65 años. Entonces, ellos, por más jóvenes que son, que busquen la tecnología y vean todo lo que pasó en Commerce, que se involucren en la historia de Commerce; para que ellos puedan saber más de la ciudad. Así es como ellos pueden compenetrarse más en esta ciudad.

¿Hay algo más que te gustaría añadir?
Algo que me gustaría añadir es que todos sigamos así, como familia, que seamos positivos, que nos conozcamos más, que no juzguemos por la primera impresión de una persona, así como me pasó a mí porque con los años te vienen a conocer todos y ya saben cómo eres.

La reina del Senior Center

Adelita Zepeda

La Reina del Senior Center

Mi nombre es Adelita Zepeda. Nací el 3 de abril del 1944 en Nayarit, México. Llegué a Los Ángeles hace 59 años y he estado viviendo en la Ciudad de Commerce hace 31 años. Primero viví en el area de Bristow y ahora en los *Senior Apartments* (apartamentos para personas mayores) desde el 2001. Antes de esto viví en el Este de Los Ángeles hasta que me quedé sola después de perder a mi esposo ya que mi hijo y mis hijas se habían casado. Cuando me lesioné y ya no pude trabajar, vine a la Ciudad de Commerce a vivir con una de mis hijas. Llevaba a mis nietos al parque de Bristow y a la biblioteca. También los llevaba a la escuela de Rosewood y veníamos al parque. Después de vivir con ella por 7 años, me mudé a los *Senior Apartments* de Rosewood. Quería ser más independiente y poder tener la libertad de hacer lo que quisiera en mi propio hogar. Ya viviendo aquí, comencé a venir a la biblioteca y al *Senior Center* (centro para personas mayores).

Cuando llegué a los *Senior Apartments*, no conocía a nadie allí porque había estado viviendo en el area de Bristow, pero como yo hablo con toda la gente, me hice amiga de unas señoras. Una se llamaba Ana y la otra Francis Soto. Una de ellas ya no vive, pero me decían, 'Adelita ¡Anímate! Vamos a los *Seniors*'. Yo les decía, 'No. Yo no conozco a nadie allí'. También mi hija me decía pero yo le dije, 'No. Yo no. ¿Cómo voy a ir al Seniors? ¡No, no, todavía no!' Al final ellas me animaron a ir al *Senior Center*.

Vivir en el area de Rosewood era como estar aislada del resto de Commerce hasta que llegaron los autobuses. Los autobuses unieron a la ciudad un poco más. Ya podía ir al area de Bristow, Bandini y Veterans. Como vivía cerca del puente sobre la autopista 5, subía el Puente para cruzar a tomar el autobús 66 en las calles Olympic y Arizona. Una vez esperando la luz verde del semáforo, un conductor que venía por la calle Arizona dio vuelta para la calle Olympic y me atropelló, aventándome a la otra banqueta.

Estuve cuatro meses en varios hospitales: Garfield Hospital, Doctor's Hospital y después en un centro de convalecencia. Cuando salí de los hospitales, tuve que ir a terapia y pensé cómo iba a ir.

En aquel entonces no teníamos los *shuttles* (minibuses) que tenemos ahora. Solo había un carro *Station Wagon* color café y un carrito blanco que me podían llevar. Cuando salí del hospital, los autobuses grandes ya estaban allí. Años después hubo autobuses y *shuttles* en la ciudad. Después de estar usando el transporte público de Commerce por 28 años, llegué a conocer muy bien a los choferes y empleados de la oficina de transportación, personas como Martita, Jaime Sandoval y Sergio. El autobús azul pasaba por mi casa y nos íbamos al supermercado El Súper. El autobús también llegaba hasta la biblioteca de Rosewood y al *Senior Center*.

En el *Senior Center* tuve varias experiencias bonitas. Durante una navidad, me nombraron reina del *Senior Center*. Yo no sabía que iban a hacer eso. En ese tiempo yo era voluntaria y estaba en la cocina con mi mandil sirviendo la comida de navidad. Me dijeron, "Adelita ven". Les dije, "¿Por qué? Yo estoy muy ocupada". Me dijeron "siéntate", así que fuí y me senté. Me di cuenta de que era porque me habían elegido para ser la reina, pero yo estaba adentro de la cocina. Me quitaron el mandil para ponerme una capa, ponerme una corona de reina y darme un ramo de flores.

Además de ser nombrada reina, también recibí un reconocimiento de la ciudad como *Senior of the Year* (Adulta Mayor del Año). Fui voluntaria de los servicios humanos por 18 años. En ese tiempo, Anne era la supervisora del *Senior Center* y Francis Esparza estaba a cargo de la comida. Yo le ayudaba a ella a registrar a la gente y a pasar la comida. Todavía soy voluntaria en el *Senior Center*, donde preparo café con galletas todos los viernes y un martes al mes. Después de eso recibí otro premio, esta vez como voluntaria del año por haber completado 750 horas de voluntariado en un año. Me llevaron a comer a un restaurante y podía invitar a seis personas. Invité a Anne, a María Rosales, "El güerito", a los dos trabajadores de los servicios humanos, a Josie Pérez, quien daba clases de flores, y a mi hija.

Aparte de ser voluntaria también fui embajadora y comisionada de biblioteca. A la biblioteca Veterans llevábamos cosas y repartíamos mochilas. Íbamos a la biblioteca con los niños a platicar. Yo tengo muchos recuerdos de estos tiempos, todos bonitos de todas las personas que conozco. Todos son número uno. Me gustan todos.

La Biblioteca Rosewood también ha crecido increíble porque no estaba tan grandota. Yo me sorprendo. Cada vez está más bonita. Me gusta mucho. Ofrece tantos servicios que son tan bonitos. Cuando puedo, yo vengo al Cafecito, un programa que tiene la Biblioteca Rosewood en el centro de alfabetización READS para ayudar a la gente a practicar inglés. Yo les digo a otras señoras todo lo que hago y las invito a venir. Antes había una chofer que se llamaba Andrea y nos traía a los Chismes Café en el *Senior Center*. Los lunes venía al club de libros en español con Yolanda a la Biblioteca Rosewood.

Así como las bibliotecas me traen buenos recuerdos, el resto de la ciudad también. En nuestros cumpleaños celebramos con una fiesta en el parque, allá afuera donde juegan básquetbol. También tuvimos eventos en las pérgolas cerca a las calles Harbor y Commerce Way. Antes se rentaban. Yo llegué a rentar para los cumpleaños de mis nietos y los míos. Se depositaba un cheque y hacías tu fiesta. Después de la fiesta te lo regresaban. Rentaban el salón al lado de la cancha de básquetbol. El costo era dependiendo de cuántas personas iban a venir. Yo encantada de la vida porque vino mi familia y todos los invitados cuando cumplí los 60 años.

La ciudad ofrece muchos servicios para los adultos mayores y también para los niños. Antes caminábamos a la biblioteca Bandini porque mi hijo vivía cerca de allí. Mi nieta trabajaba en el *Senior Center* como parte del *YES Program* (un programa educativo y de servicios para los jóvenes). Mi nieta de 10 años está en un grupo de baile folclórico. Le encanta el baile a ella. Acaba de hacer una presentación del Cinco de mayo muy bonita.

Recuerdo que antes había un lugar que se llamaba Lucky's, pero ahora es El Súper. También había Thrifty, donde vendían las nieves. Me hace falta porque cuando terminaba en el *Senior Center* me agarraba el autobús y ahí me bajaba, pero ya quitaron dos paradas del autobús. Cambiaron las paradas de los autobuses y los números. Con el tiempo todo ha cambiado. Antes todo era más chico. Había menos población, menos movimiento y no teníamos tanta transportación de los autobuses grandes. Tampoco teníamos paseos y ahora ya tenemos hasta tres o cuatro paseos al mes.

Hay tantos recuerdos bonitos de la ciudad. Espero que podamos conservar bien todo lo que tenemos, que los jóvenes que viven aquí aprovechen, que vayan a jugar básquetbol y que hagan ejercicios. Tenemos muchas máquinas en el parque. Deseo que sigan sus estudios porque también tenemos cuatro bibliotecas que pueden visitar.

A la gente que no sabe nada de la Ciudad de Commerce les digo que vengan, que se involucren, que hablen con las personas y que pregunten si no saben. Hay volantes de diferentes cosas, calendarios de eventos mensuales de la biblioteca, el *Senior Center* y viajes.

Estoy muy contenta con todos los servicios que tenemos en nuestra ciudad. Espero que sigamos conservandola limpia porque es nuestra casa. Para mí es mi casa. El *Senior Center* es mi segunda casa. Acá vengo tres o cuatro días a la semana. Me gusta tanto mi ciudad. Yo la quiero mucho.

Madre, comunidad y el arte de dar

Carmen Mancilla

Madre, comunidad y el arte de dar

Antes de ser voluntaria y de trabajar en la biblioteca, incluso antes de sentirse parte de una ciudad, Carmen Mancilla fue madre. Desde ese lugar —el más exigente y el más generoso— comenzó su relación con la Ciudad de Commerce.

Carmen llegó a Commerce como llegan muchas madres trabajadoras: buscando estabilidad, espacio y oportunidades para una familia que crecía. Durante años combinó la vida laboral con la crianza de sus hijos con esfuerzo. Como tantas madres, su tiempo era limitado, pero su compromiso era profundo. Cada decisión que tomaba estaba guiada por una pregunta constante: ¿qué es lo mejor para mis hijos?

Commerce se convirtió en el escenario donde sus hijos crecieron. La ciudad les ofreció algo invaluable: programas deportivos, clases de natación y actividades que llenaban sus días de estructura y propósito. Para Carmen, estas oportunidades no eran solo recreación; eran una extensión de la educación que ella daba en casa. Mantener a sus hijos activos, acompañados y rodeados de comunidad era una forma de cuidado y de amor.

Ser madre también le enseñó a mirar más allá de su propio hogar. Cuando sus hijos comenzaron a crecer, Carmen sintió el deseo de agradacer a la ciudad por lo que le había dado. Buscó espacios para servir, no solo para ayudar, sino para mostrarles a sus hijos que formar parte de una comunidad implica responsabilidad y gratitud. Dar no era una obligación; era un valor.

Ese camino la llevó a la biblioteca. Primero comenzó como voluntaria en el programa *Homebound*, luego como Embajadora de la Biblioteca y, con el tiempo, como parte del personal. La biblioteca se convirtió en un punto de encuentro entre su vida como madre y su vocación de servicio. Allí aprendió, enseñó y acompañó a otros, mientras sus hijos observaban de cerca el ejemplo de una madre que servía a su comunidad con constancia.

Carmen no solo hablaba de dar; lo practicaba. Sus hijos crecieron viéndola trabajar, servir y comprometerse con los demás. A través de su ejemplo, aprendieron que una ciudad no es solo un lugar donde se vive, sino un espacio que se cuida y se construye entre todos.

A lo largo de los años, Carmen fue testiga de los cambios en Commerce, pero también fue parte de aquello que no cambia: el valor de una madre que trabaja duro, que participa y que enseña con el ejemplo. Para ella, la biblioteca representa ese espíritu: un lugar donde el conocimiento se comparte, donde nadie queda fuera y donde siempre hay algo que aprender.

Hoy, al mirar atrás, Carmen se siente orgullosa no solo de su trabajo o de su voluntariado, sino de haber criado a sus hijos en una ciudad que les permitió crecer con oportunidades y valores. Su historia es la de muchas madres, pero también es única: una historia de esfuerzo, comunidad y generosidad heredada.

La historia de Carmen Mancilla nos recuerda que las ciudades no se sostienen solo con edificios o programas, sino con mujeres como Carmen, que enseñan, día a día, que dar de regreso es también una forma de hogar.

Una ciudad llamada "Comercio"

Ana Luisa Holton

Una ciudad llamada "Comercio"

Ana Luisa Holton no nació en la Ciudad de Commerce, pero con el tiempo su corazón decidió quedarse ahí. Vivió muchos años en el Este de Los Ángeles, tan cerca de Commerce, que la calle donde vivía terminaba justo donde comenzaba la ciudad. Aun así, no fue la cercanía lo que la conquistó. Fue algo mucho más profundo: la manera en que la ciudad la hizo sentir.

La primera vez que escuchó el nombre Ciudad de Commerce le causó curiosidad. Le sonó contradictorio. Una ciudad llamada "comercio", pero lo que ella veía no tenía nada de frío ni de industrial. Veía un pueblo, un lugar tranquilo, latino, lleno de vida con flores en las calles, vecinos que se saludan y una energía amable.

Un día, caminando sin rumbo, avanzó un poco más de lo habitual y se topó con la Biblioteca del Parque Bristow. Se detuvo, sonrió y en ese instante lo supo.

"Las bibliotecas son mi segunda casa", dice. "Me fascina estar en la biblioteca." Ahí fue cuando se enamoró de Commerce.

Poco después, vio pasar un autobús que decía City of Commerce. Pensó que sería pequeño y sencillo, pero se sorprendió: era cómodo, bonito y bien cuidado. Para ella, eso decía mucho. Decía que era una ciudad pensada para su gente, una ciudad que cuida.

Con el tiempo empezó a hacer amigas. Una de ellas la invitó a una actividad en la Biblioteca Central de Commerce. Ana Luisa se enamoró. No solo encontró libros. Encontró personas. Encontró calidez. Encontró programas en español. Encontró poesía y, cuando supo que habría una clase de poesía, sintió que algo se acomodaba dentro de ella.

"Yo escribo poesía", pensó.

"Entonces, esta sí es mi casa."

Desde ese momento, la Ciudad de Commerce se volvió su lugar, su refugio y su espacio seguro. Los libros la trajeron. La gente la hizo quedarse.

Ana Luisa es poeta, y eso se nota en la forma en que observa
el mundo. Recuerda con emoción una actividad en la biblioteca
donde el coordinador del programa, Juan Fabrius, los invitó a
cerrar los ojos, escuchar los sonidos y escribir a partir de ellos.
Para ella fue algo mágico, tan mágico que después llevó esa
experiencia a sus propios espacios de poesía. Commerce no sólo
la recibió. La inspiró.

Ella siente que la gente de la Ciudad de Commerce es distinta.

Más amable.
Más tranquila.
Más luminosa.
"Como las flores", dice.

Aquí también descubrió otra de sus pasiones: los mercados. Los
mercados de pulgas, los de antigüedades, los farmers markets.
Cuando encontró uno en el Parque Rosewood, se sintió en casa.
Salió feliz, con el corazón lleno y la camioneta casi repleta de
plantas y pequeños tesoros.

Ha visto cambios, claro. La biblioteca se renovó. La población creció. Hay más movimiento, más gente y más vida. Para ella, eso es
algo bueno. "Hay más alegría y más luz", dice.

Ana Luisa no nació en Commerce, pero cuando uno adopta un lugar, lo ama de verdad. Habla del Citadel Outlets como uno de sus
espacios favoritos para caminar, respirar y disfrutar sin sentirse
encerrada. Para ella, Commerce es libertad, es espacio y es aire.

Cuando habla de los niños, su voz se suaviza. Recuerda haber
visto a un adulto mayor sentado en la alfombra de la biblioteca,
conversando con pequeños. Para ella, eso es sagrado. Eso es
hogar.

"Un niño que se siente seguro, crece feliz", dice.

Casi siempre sale de la Biblioteca de la Ciudad de Commerce
cargando libros para regalar, compartir y sembrar un futuro. Cree
profundamente que un libro es esperanza, abre caminos y puede

cambiar una vida. Ella misma ha adoptado una familia de niños a quienes les lleva libros siempre porque quiere que sueñen, que crezcan y que crean.

Ana Luisa cree en la comunidad, en la unión y en la fuerza de estar juntos. Cree que los jóvenes deben saber que este país también es suyo, que nadie les apague los sueños, que estudien, que luchen, que crezcan y que hagan de Commerce un lugar aún más mejor.

Cuando habla de identidad, su voz se vuelve firme.
Ella es guatemalteca.
Es centroamericana.
Es estadounidense.
Es americana.

Y lo dice con orgullo.

Para Ana Luisa, América no es sólo un país, es un continente, es su gente, personas que trabajan, que aman y que aportan. Cree que los latinos traen cultura, alegría, fuerza y luz. Siente que Commerce, con sus bibliotecas, sus parques, su transporte, su educación y su calidez, está haciendo su parte.

"Este país es nuestro", ella dice. "Y los niños tienen derecho a crecer felices aquí."

Life in Commerce

Luis Sandoval

Life in Commerce

I had memories of the City of Commerce before I even moved to California. Memories of my first visit to Commerce are vague, but I do remember visiting for Christmas or summer. Most days were joyful while other days involved family conflicts. During my time in Commerce, I realized how different it was compared to where I had lived during the time, in Tacoma, Washington.

When visiting Commerce, we would go to the beach, mall, or stay inside my grandparents' house. I remember being given a pogo stick on Christmas Day and I didn't stop using it until we had to return home; there were also embarrassing moments, like the time I slipped and fell off the back of the truck! After years of visiting, I finally moved to Commerce and was greeted with feelings of nostalgia. But I realized that I had to make new memories and discover more.

The hospitality around Commerce was comfortable enough to feel safe walking around the neighborhood. It was easier speaking to the people; it was as if everyone was close to each other. The difference between both states is noticeable, to the people and the diversity, areas to go walk or shop, the culture, and much more. The city looks its best when decorated for Christmas.

I had more fun being out in Commerce than I ever had when I lived in Tacoma. The community of Commerce is memorable enough to where I wish they did some of the activities they did in the past. Some events held in Commerce took place at Rosewood Park where they celebrated the 4th of July with a fair, hunting eggs on Easter, movie nights, and other small activities. The library near the park was unique. People could borrow games, hang around, or use computers.

Commerce has faced some difficult times. Everyone knew everyone before COVID and after that, the city seemed to have no one around the area from being quarantined. But things are improving. Since COVID, the city has been adding more to its area. There have been reports of them adding Chick Fil-A and In n Out right near Citadel and Jack in the Box near Bandini. This brings more people to the community, who experience a good time. There are many people who would welcome the opportunity to live in Commerce.

Moving to Commerce was probably the best decision my family made. I wouldn't be the person I am today, had I not made the friends I did, and shared experiences with them. Commerce is becoming more well-known and I'd love to see more people join us.

My Memories in Commerce
Schurr High School Student

My Memories in Commerce

My family moved to Commerce on April 17, 2009, when I was barely turning 2. My first ever memory was in a pool at the Brenda Villa Aquatic Center. I was playing around with my brother and all the other little kids near me. Since I already knew how to swim, it was child's play to me. I didn't really like the small pool even though it was made for small children like me; I would always complain about being in that small pool. I really liked being in the bigger pools; they are deeper, better to swim, and I had so much more room to roam around that I felt like I could breathe because no one was in my personal space.

I started swimming when I was very young. I would swim all the time and I really liked it because it was something I was very good at– and no one could tell me I wasn't! That's where no one could bully me. I wasn't the "loser" or the "fat girl". When I was with my team and coach, I was Jaz; I was treated like a human being with feelings for once. I've always loved to swim. It was my safe place and still is. When I started doing more activities at Commerce, it was life changing– especially when my mom took us to Camp Commerce for the first time.

I was 7-years-old when I first went to Camp Commerce and my family didn't know that we were supposed to bring our own pillows, so we slept very badly. Now when we go, I overpack just in case I need something I didn't think about. My most memorable moment was when the camp staff took everyone in the camp to Lake Arrowhead, we went canoeing, and the staff asked us if we wanted to jump off the dock into the lake and no one volunteered. Only I did. It was so much fun and after I jumped, others jumped too. Another memorable moment in camp was when I would make paintings, bracelets, and keychains for my mom; she still keeps them till this day.

The camp closed when COVID hit, as did a lot of other things that made the city fun, like the pool and the snack bar. I had a lot of good memories in the snack bar, too. That's where my mom worked, where my middle school friends and I would eat and hangout, and where my sister and I used to hangout.

The City of Commerce really impacted me and my way of looking at things, especially Camp Commerce. I want to live there. It was, and still is, the greatest thing that has ever happened to me. When I would go in the winter the air was always so fresh, the scenery beautiful, and it would make me feel really happy. I love going with my mom because when we're there, the air is always more fresh and the camp is more peaceful.

Commerce: A Friendly Place
Schurr High School Student

Commerce: A Friendly Place

When I was around nine years old, we moved to a new house in the City of Commerce. I have this weird memory of sitting in a little red chair, in an empty room, and looking out the window. I was kinda scared but also kinda excited, too! My school was super close, which was cool, and my parents would drive us, but I remember wanting to walk with my brother. He was like "no way man, I'm not taking you with me," but whatever; I started to like Commerce a lot; it wasn't so bad after all.

Commerce is a friendly place. Aside from the fun events in the park, are the super nice neighbors. When we first moved in, my dad was sick. They helped us out a lot. As time went on, they would watch our house and even have birthday parties with us. It made Commerce not so scary. I really love Commerce; if you ever come to Commerce, I would totally show you our park!

Living near the Citadel Outlets is awesome. I can get snacks or go shopping super quick. During the holidays, we always walk there, so we don't get stuck in traffic. The park and the library are super close, too. I go to park events all the time and I even got a school prize because I live in Commerce. It's pretty sweet. Once we attended a park celebration of the Fourth of July. There were games, and food, and fireworks! It was so much fun. All my friends were there and we stayed up super late watching the fireworks. It was like the best night ever!

Then there's the library; I love going to the library! They have so many books and computers. I always do my homework there and sometimes I just go there to read; it's a really cool place to hang out.

Commerce is always doing stuff to make the city better. They're building new stuff and fixing up old stuff. It's really cool to see the city change and grow. I think Commerce is going to be even better in the future! I remember when they first built the park, it was just an empty lot and now it's this amazing place, with playgrounds, sports fields, and walking trails. It's so cool to see how much it's changed.

The people in Commerce are so nice. Everyone is always smiling and saying hello; it's a really friendly community. I've lived in Commerce for a long time now and I feel really lucky to live here. I can't imagine living anywhere else. The people are great. They care about each other and work together to make it a better place. I'm really proud to be a part of it.

I'm glad I moved here when I was little. It turned out to be the best thing ever! Commerce has really grown on me; it's not just a place I live, it's a part of who I am. I've made so many memories here and I'm excited to see what the future holds for Commerce and for me.

Growing Up With Commerce

Alexander Rodríguez

Growing up with Commerce

When I think about Commerce, California, I think about my dad. He is 68 years old now and even though he lives in Montebello today, his childhood and teenage years were all spent in Commerce. Back then the city looked nothing like it does now. It was still being built and it felt like the streets and buildings were growing up right alongside him.

He has told me so many stories about what life was like in those early days. Commerce was just getting started and a lot of the streets were still made of dirt. There were open lots everywhere and not many stores or businesses yet. He would ride his bike through areas that were still under construction and he remembers watching buildings slowly go up around him. It felt like the whole city was a big project that he was somehow part of just by living there.

One place that really meant a lot to him was the Commerce Public Library. He said when it first opened, it felt like entering another world. He would go there after school and spend hours reading and exploring new ideas. It became a safe space for him, a place where he could dream bigger than what was around him. That love of learning stayed with him, even after he moved away, and it is something he passed down to me.

He remembers how close everyone was in the community. People knew their neighbors and helped each other out. If someone needed something people showed up. He talks about the small local businesses and how they treated every customer like family. As the city grew more, people moved in but that sense of connection never really went away. Even now, when we visit, you can still feel that community spirit in the way people treat one another.

My dad saw Commerce change year after year. He remembers when the city started holding small parades and community events. At first they were simple and small but they brought people together and made the city feel alive. He also remembers the parks being built and how excited the kids were to have places to play. When the city introduced free bus rides it made a big difference for a lot of families. It gave people the chance to get around without worrying about money and it brought more freedom and opportunity to everyone.

Even though he moved to Montebello years ago, he still talks about Commerce with a lot of love. It shaped him in so many ways. He learned how to work hard, how to care about people and how to stay connected to the world around him. He did not just live in the city while it was growing, he lived through its most important changes. That makes his story a big part of the city's story too.

To me, Commerce is more than a city on a map. It is a place full of memories and lessons. It is where my dad grew up and where he learned to become the person he is today. The streets and buildings may look different now but they hold pieces of his past and the lives of so many people who helped build the city into what it is. If someone asks me what makes Commerce special, I would say it is the people who believed in it and grew with it, people like my dad.

My Life in Commerce, California

Marliza García Torres

My Life in Commerce, California

Commerce, California is more than just a place where I live, it's a place that helped shape who I am. Even though it's a small city, it's full of strong memories, kind people, and opportunities that have helped me grow. I may not have always noticed it, but looking back, I can see how much this city has done for me and my family. From school to community events and even just daily life, Commerce has always been a place where I felt safe and connected.

One of my favorite memories in Commerce is spending time at the Citadel Outlets. I remember one summer day when my family and I went shopping there. It was warm outside, and the place was full of people from all over. We didn't even buy much that day—we were mostly just walking around, laughing, and enjoying the cool stores and food. I remember eating Wetzel's Pretzels and sitting by the fountain watching the lights glow as it got dark. That simple day stuck with me because it was full of happiness and no stress. It showed me that the Citadel is more than just a shopping center—it's a place where people come together. Even if we're not buying anything, just being there creates memories.

My family moved to Commerce for better schools and safer neighborhoods. When we got here, it felt quiet but welcoming. Over time, I realized how lucky I was to grow up in a city that cares about its people. The schools are well-supported, and there are many programs for kids and teens. As I got older, I noticed how involved the community is, especially during events like the Fourth of July Fireworks Show or the Christmas Tree Lighting near City Hall. These events aren't just fun—they bring people together and remind us that we're part of something special.

The people in Commerce are friendly, and many of them have lived here their whole lives. It feels like a small town where everyone knows each other, even though we're close to a big city like Los Angeles. One of my favorite things is how the city supports kids with after-school programs, sports leagues, and the Teen Center. It gives us a place to go, stay safe, and have fun. There are also parks, libraries, and community buses that help people who don't drive get around easily. The free bus system is something most cities don't have, and it shows how much Commerce cares about its residents.

Living in Commerce has helped me become the person I am today. It's taught me about community, kindness, and working hard. I've had chances to grow, meet good people, and stay focused on my goals.

The city encourages young people to stay busy and stay out of trouble. Whether it's playing sports or just using the library, there's always something to do.

I'm proud to be from Commerce. I know it's not the biggest city, and maybe not everyone knows where it is, but I do—and it matters to me. If I had to explain Commerce to someone who has never been here, I would say it's a small city with a big heart. It's a place where people look out for each other, and where you can make real memories—like walking through the Citadel with your family, watching the lights flicker at night.

Commerce isn't just my hometown. It's a part of who I am. It's given me chances, experiences, and a strong sense of belonging. I'll always carry that with me, no matter where I go. Whether I'm walking through the Citadel, riding the city bus, or just hanging out at a local event, I know that Commerce has helped shape my identity. It has shown me the importance of community, support, and pride in where you come from. Even if I leave one day to explore new places or chase my dreams, I'll never forget the memories I made here. Commerce will always feel like home, and I'll always be thankful for everything this city has taught me.

Commerce Now
Published by City of Commerce Public Library

Director of Library Services
Sonia Bautista

Project Coordinators
Erik Jackiw, Adult Services Librarian
Josué Martínez, Senior Library Assistant
Silvia Cisneros, Senior Librarian
Vanessa Manzanárez, Adult Services Librarian
Erica López, Owner of Daxson Publishing

Book Cover
Josué Martínez

City Council
Kevin Lainez, Mayor
Mireya García, Mayor Pro Tem
Hugo A. Argumedo, Councilmember
Ivan Altamirano, Councilmember
Oralia Y. Rebollo, Councilmember